Burek

A Culinary Metaphor

Jernej
Mlekuž

Central European University Press
Budapest–New York

Translated from Slovene by Peter Altshul
with support from the Slovenian Book Agency.

Published in 2015 by
Central European University Press
An imprint of the
Central European University Limited Liability Company
Nádor utca 11, H-1051 Budapest, Hungary
Tel: +36-1-327-3138 or 327-3000
Fax: +36-1-327-3183
E-mail: ceupress@press.ceu.edu
Website: www.ceupress.com

224 West 57th Street, New York, NY 10019, USA
Tel: +1-212-547-6932
Fax: +1-646-557-2416
E-mail: meszarosa@press.ceu.edu

ISBN 978-963-386-089-2 Cloth
ISBN 978-963-386-090-8 Paperback

Printed in Hungary
Prime Rate Kft., Budapest

Library of Congress Cataloging-in-Publication Data

Mlekuž, Jernej.
Burek : a culinary metaphor / Jernej Mlekuž.
pages cm
Includes bibliographical references and index.
ISBN 978-9633860908 (hardbound : alk. paper)
1. Discourse analysis--Slovenia. 2. Political culture--Slovenia. 3. Popular culture--Slovenia. 4. Nationalism--Slovenia. 5. Immigrants--Slovenia--Public opinion. 6. Pies--Slovenia. 7. Food--Symbolic aspects--Slovenia. 8. Metaphor--Political aspects--Slovenia. 9. Slovenia--Politics and government. 10. Slovenia--Social life and customs. I. Title.
P302.15.S57M54 2015
306.4429184--dc23

2014046043

Contents

List of Figures

Foreburek

(I Mean: Foreword)

It is entirely clear where the greatest difficulty lies in researching the burek. It is in the gap that separates the inferior status of the research subject in the eyes of the average academician and the exceptional success of the burek in the nutritional strategies, the speech and the imagination of the inhabitants of Slovenia.

This success on its own effectively demands that we entertain the burek as seriously as we would any weighty subject. But the disparity between the burek's practical success and its theoretical obscurity poses two related requirements with regard to researching—and particularly writing about—the burek. The first is the requirement for academic reflection: one has to consider the heterogeneity of the ontogeny of the burek as an object and a research topic. The second is the requirement that the writing justifies the research approach and that the reflection is used to translate the disparity into a focused narrative.

How successful Jernej Mlekuž was at navigating these waters will be for the readers to decide; it would not be appropriate to act like a television anchor and summarize the entire text in a sound bite. But we can illustrate what it's all about briefly and simply in a few paragraphs.

The object itself, whether you are speaking of one whose delicious smell is wafting from your oven at home or one that they are wrapping all hot and greasy in paper so you can eat it on the run while doing errands in the city, is nothing new. Similar dishes have been prepared in the Pannonian part of Slovenia for centuries, although they did not call it a "burek." But the newcomers who brought the word itself to Slovenia, when they began selling bureks in kiosks near railway and bus stations or military barracks, reserve the name for the limited number of items that are referred to by that name in Slovenia today.

Thus, the very notions of the identity and origin of the burek are problematic: what is and what is not a burek; is it a native or an immigrant?

This dilemma can be considered in several ways. Let's start slowly and finish with more salt: did our grandmothers already know how to make bureks, or did we learn how to make them at home only after getting used to enjoying them on the street, as a part of student life and an indisputably urban experience, but in each case as a powerful generator of later nostalgia for our youth?

There is no speaking or writing about the burek that is not as saturated with the subject than the burek is nutritionally and linguistically saturated with burek grease. "Saturated with the subject": I worked hard to choose those precise words. The idea presented in the preceding two paragraphs cannot be transliterated as: "the burek as a material object is appropriated by various ideologies" (or various discourses), or as: "our relationship to the burek is mediated by personal experiences" (or filtered through history, culture, memory or something even hazier). In both cases, it would be as if the burek was something immanent, over which various behaviours or beliefs fight, when it is already here. In the first case, with the ideologies, there would be the additional danger of annihilating the materiality of the burek by seeing it merely as an amalgamation of external determinations. In the second case we would merely be replacing the relative objectivity of a sociological reduction with a less specific and more generalized reduction through which the burek would be assigned a fate just like any other object: we use it and speak about it, but both change through space and time. How educational!

If however I state that the burek is saturated with the subject, I at least indicate that our relationship to the burek cannot be broken down into prefactors, since it is a component of our fantasies, and not just our diets. The burek is a subject of consumption (enjoyment) not just in the culinary, but especially in the psychoanalytical sense.

"You're a burek," or "you don't have enough for a burek"; "Burek? Nein, danke." Only by considering the scope of this consumption can we appreciate the reasons for the inseparability of speechifying about the burek from the material practice of its production, distribution, and consumption. We enjoy the burek in our language much more than on our palates.

The burek is therefore an excellent thing to think about, since it has landed where we eat. It has crept its way into the place of pizzas and hamburgers, if we are talking about fast food. It has crept its way into the place of tripe or goulash, if we are talking about hot snacks. It has smuggled its way to a privileged position as a densely construed metaphor for the Balkans in Slovenian usage—a place which for Štih in the eighties was held by čevapčiči. Without the burek it would be similarly difficult to contemplate the jargon of Slovenian youth, the world of the imagination of Slovenian chauvinism and the rhetorical arsenal of health food advertising agents.

Therefore it was both necessary and high time that Slovenian humanities and social science, through the agency of Jernej Mlekuž, dealt with the burek: not just one more thing among many, but something which via speech has saturated everything. Could we say that it wasn't true if we woke up tomorrow and saw graffiti on a neighbouring wall that said: "Everything is burek!"?

Well, this is more than enough for a foreword. Let the author have the floor.

Jože Vogrinc
Professor of Philosophy
University of Ljubljana

Preburek

I usually don't have any trouble understanding and adhering to the rules, conventions, stability and everything else from the world of the self-evident. So I should say right at the beginning that my intention in writing this book was not to dig up a pile of difficulties, unpleasantness and other horrors. This, however, would not be easy, at least for this undertaking, and I am not at all convinced that I succeeded. So where are these unexpected and, at least in this frightfully serious place, wholly unwelcome difficulties hiding?

The difficulties arise from its ordained status, i.e. the reason for writing this book.[1] This is supposed to be a scientific text, is it not? But Aristotle himself noted that the scope of human affairs is not controlled by eternal principles and necessities—in this realm, things can be "one way or another." In this realm, therefore, true knowledge is not possible; only prudence is.[2] The situation is even worse, since my field is none other than the interpretation of human affairs, which could by definition be said to be subject to human interpretation. If I therefore accept at the outset that things can be "one way or another," and thus abandon the illusion that I could turn my efforts into a workshop of exact science, I quickly find myself faced with a none-too-pleasant question:

---

1 This theme was first addressed in my doctoral thesis entitled "Predmet kot akter? Primer bureka v Sloveniji" [Object as Actor? The Case of the Burek in Slovenia] (University of Nova Gorica, 2008).

2 In my interpretation and summarizing of Chapters 5 and 6 of Book VI of Aristotle's *The Nicomachean Ethics* (trans. by Harris Rackham [Cambridge, MA: Harvard University Press, 1934), 337–341, I was greatly aided by Rastko Močnik "Studia humanitatis danes" [Studia Humanitatis Today], in *Retorika Starih / Elementi semiologije* [Anicent Rhetoric / Elements of Semiology], by Roland Barthes (Ljubljana: Studia humanitatis, 1990), 217–218. This work was also of great help to me in articulating this onerous question.

can my supposedly "scientific" task—the interpretation of these human affairs—be anything other than non-scientific, i.e. everyday interpretive human behaviour? Other than my subject itself and humanities research in general?[3]

From this ominous, fearsome, vexatious question—which has haunted me throughout the entire task—straight to practical, technical ones, ones that are of personal interest to me—about which, in fact, there isn't a lot to say. How should I even begin this introductory chapter? Should I give away some of the contents? And if so, how much so it won't immediately be too much, so that not everything will be clear to the reader before they get a whiff of the later chapters, more redolent of bureks? Well, I'll give it a shot. What choice do I have?

"Preburek"! However metaphysical that may sound, this preface is given to strictly technical issues. That is, I threw everything into it that is not directly related to bureks. Well, except for the hypothesis.[4]

In the chapter "Towards the Burek," which follows this preface, I define the frameworks of the analysis of the burek, or the metaburek. The metaburek? That's right. It is in some sense the burek's superstructure, to borrow Karl Marx's architecture. And if you are hungry for more I can recommend the following chapter, "About the Burek."

The title of that chapter pretty much says it all. Is there anything to add? Well, the fact that it is followed by the "Afterburek," which concludes the "textual" part of this book.

This is followed by the "non-textual" part, (Non-)Burekliterature and the "Burekarchive," about which there is also not a lot to say.

Or is there? As a matter of fact I have forgotten to mention that to

3 I will list just one of the great ideas that could help us, albeit indirectly, answer the above question: "It is therefore better, instead of contrasting magic and science, to compare them as two parallel modes of acquiring knowledge. Their theoretical and practical results differ in value ... [but] require the same sort of mental operations and they differ not so much in kind as in the different types of phenomena to which they are applied." (Claude Lévi-Strauss, *The Savage Mind*, trans. George Weidenfeld [Chicago: The University of Chicago Press, 1966], 13.) To summarize very freely: people have always known how to think well, not just since the advent of science.

4 The hypothesis of, or more accurately the question posed by this book is: It seems completely redundant to say that the burek is not just food, not merely something to fill your belly with, not just a physiological necessity. It's a lot more than that! But what in fact is this "more"—the super-burek, the metaburek—and how should it be understood, approached, analyzed?

a great extent I was led to the burek and that my thinking about the burek was guided by Michel Foucault. The name which appears most frequently in the textual part of the book. And in the textual part he is probably the winner. Which is not in fact all that important. Owing to my respect for the most frequently-cited person in this book, I have to say that I have often understood and used him quite freely. Perhaps even abused him.[5] But "the birth of the reader must be at the cost of the death of the author," as Roland Barthes ruthlessly concludes while discussing the discourse of (who else?) Foucault.[6] A text has significantly more meanings than those intended or desired by the author. When an author sends his work out into the world, its meaning is no longer dependent solely on him; it has its own life. Its meaning is found in various contexts and is subject to various interpretations.

Actually, I wanted to say something else with regard to Foucault. I don't believe my book contains anything greatly original, exceptional or creative. And this lack of originality does not stem only from the fact that "[the] frontiers of a book are never clear-cut: beyond the title, the first lines, and the last full stop, beyond its internal configuration and its autonomous form, it is caught up in a system of references to other books, other texts, other sentences." It is not only due to the fact that the text before you is a "node within a network," as Foucault concludes this metaphor.[7] It is also or even mainly about the burek (although I did say that this chapter doesn't contain any burekspeak), which is not just some substance to be used as a lay illustration of some a priori concept. It is a substance that also structures, conceptualizes, and imagines the word itself. It is life, if I may indulge in a slightly inflated form of expression, trapped in a (biocentrically speaking) non-living body, which

5 In the process of thinking, reading and writing I have also encountered numerous contradictions and inconsistencies in Foucault's thought, which I have not specifically exposed. My eclectic approach is based on the inclusion of the concepts used, and not on their analysis, discussion and criticism. I have no intention of depriving the author of his greatness, which he earned, in my opinion justifiably, because of his exceptional cognitive adventurousness, intellectual nonconformity and acuity. Recognizing his greatness of course does not constitute idolatry.

6 Roland Barthes, "The Death of the Author," in *Image—Music—Text*, selected and trans. Stephen Heath (London: Fontana Press, 1977), 148.

7 Michel Foucault, *The Archaeology of Knowledge*, trans. A. M. Sheridan Smith (London; New York: Routledge, 2002), 25–26.

is undoubtedly more interesting due to its own existence than to the conceptual, stylistic and other approaches of the writer. Any originality should therefore be attributed to the burek itself.

And even if I ignore the object of analysis by making it passive, weak and unimportant to the creation of this text and to culture, society and the world in general, the authorship of texts is not raised like some divine phenomenon above this world to a heavenly, consecrated world of the chosen:

> *We can easily imagine a culture where discourses could circulate without any need for an author. Discourses, whatever their status, form, or value, and regardless of our manner of handling them, would unfold in a pervasive anonymity. No longer the tiresome repetitions: "Who is the real author? Have we proof of his authenticity and originality? What has he revealed of his most profound self in his language?" New questions will be heard: "What are the modes of existence of this discourse? Where does it come from; how is it circulated; who controls it? What placements are determined for possible subjects? Who can fulfil these diverse functions of the subject?" Behind all the questions we would hear little more that the murmur of indifference: "What matter who's speaking?"*[8]

With a generous amount of interpretive freedom I could summarize this idea and adapt it to the needs of this text: I am well aware that this text is a document, a child of its time; at the same time I very quietly, solemnly, hoping for a miracle, add: maybe, just possibly, a little more.

Finally—after these pathetic words, which like to parade around in such introductions, so that, as the unwritten rule dictates, we have to remove them from serious scientific treatises—some more or less technical data and caveats.

A bit more on writing: most often in the sciences a self-evident process, a necessary evil, unworthy of excessive reflection, which on the

8 Michel Foucault, "What is an Author?" in *Language, Counter-memory, Practice: Selected Essays and Interviews by Michel Foucault*, ed. Donald F. Bouchard (New York: Cornell University Press, 1980), 138.

other hand consumes copious amounts of time. A tortuously enjoyable process, which leads both writers and readers into mirth and disgust. A not necessarily manageable process, which in this adventure of mine proved to be a particularly bold voyager which often quite unexpectedly took off in directions that I couldn't have imagined in my wildest thoughts. But: I write, therefore I am.[9]

However, I actually wanted to say something about style. A lot of people would fervently and also probably somewhat exasperatedly claim that style is not appropriate for this type of work. A scientific study! But I must admit that my use of a more "relaxed," less formal style was to a great extent intentional.[10] Scientific writing somewhat unavoidably demands the use of elitist, exclusivist professional jargon, which the scientist uses as an index of his professional knowledge. That is, there is a sort of convention at work here, an unwritten rule, which dictates a conformist use of scientific language. As John Fiske (and very likely many others) has established, the exclusivity of various professional vocations is to a great extent a consequence of the use of special language, often incomprehensible to others, or to put it academically, restricted codes.[11] In my humble opinion, the use of these restricted codes, of this professional, exclusivist language, is frequently excessive and unnecessary. It

9 But writing wasn't the only noteworthy process in this scientific endeavour. In the spring of 2005 I began collecting burekstatements—everything that was actually published or materialized about the burek in various forms—which I still more or less faithfully continue to do today, after the last sentence has been written. I will list only the a few of the most common places where the expressions appeared: websites, periodicals and other print publications, conversations (over the telephone, on computer screens, face to face and even some in which I was not directly involved, but merely observed), literature, popular and other music, city walls (graffiti), films, plays. Collecting these heterogeneous, diffuse, (in)visible expressions involved various approaches and strategies (I am reluctant to call them "scientific" methods): reviewing, scanning, surfing websites, searching periodicals (most often in those that are also published online and thus allow "fast" searching using keywords—in my case "burek"!), films, literature; conversations, or more precisely searching for and activating burekstatements in speech acts (this was occasionally noticeable in my dictating of conversations through clearly posed and direct questions, while at other times I preferred to listen and allow the conversations to proceed naturally, sometimes even without my active participation—i.e., participant observation). This confused, relaxed, non-exclusive collecting of burekstatements inevitably also included my friends, colleagues, advisor, wife, and others. Thus in my project rather than methodology it would be more reasonable and necessary to speak of an "anti-methodology." I offer this paraphrase of Paul Feyerabend's *Against Method* (London: Verso, 1975) together with his critical approach and above all his mischievousness.

10 To put it more professionally and precisely, I employ elements of linguistic style among which both word formation (e.g. compounds) and textual elements (e.g. interjections) stand out.

11 John Fiske, *Introduction to Communication Studies* (London: Routledge, 1990), 76.

often seems that it only results or succeeds in emphasizing the dissociation from others, the non-professional and uneducated, and confirming membership in the professional, scientific elite. I do not mean to say that scientific language is merely empty "form" without content, just one of many codes that could be substituted with another code without major difficulties or consequences. Science, however we understand it, has to renounce the veneration of exclusivist "forms," and should strive not for restricted codes but elaborated ones—but of course not to the detriment of "content" and not on behalf of the present-day version of the Golden Calf: popularization. Only in this way can science demonstrate or prove that the "form" does not conceal an empty space, but "content."

Therefore I admit (and perhaps there is a bit of self-praise in it) that I wrote this text for several audiences. I wrote it so that it could be read by both the enlightened (people with PhDs) and the unenlightened (people without estimable titles), burekeaters and non-burekeaters, burek fans and inquisitors, bureknovices and burekconnoisseurs. And my fear of this motley horde was overcome by the entertaining thought of how some would burn the text at the stake while others would defend it with swords. But a description of such leisure-time activities, as they often very significantly characterized my scientific endeavours, and such colourful language have no place in a serious scientific text. Or perhaps they do if they are used against it...[12]

And a warning, which should not be taken lightly: Beware! After consuming this text, the burek will never be the same! So let's get going...

---

12 Just one morsel from the pen of one of the thinkers who respond to the above question in the negative: "A person's religion, for example, or his metaphysics, or his sense of humour (his natural sense of humour and not the inbred and always rather nasty kind of jocularity one finds in specialized professions) must not have the slightest connection with his scientific activity. His imagination is restrained, and even his language ceases to be his own. This is again reflected in the nature of scientific 'facts' which are experienced as being independent of opinion, belief, and cultural background. It is thus *possible* to create a tradition that is held together by strict rules, and that is also successful to some extent. But is it *desirable* to support such a tradition to the exclusion of everything else?" (Feyerabend, *Against Method*, 19.) Along with the author of these lines, I respond: no!

Towards the Burek

The Burek and the Metaburek

> *FIRST-RATE BUREKS, apple and cheese for 180 dinars, meat for 220 dinars, have been available for some time at the kiosk in front of the Metropol hotel. So far there have been no complaints about the service, cleanliness or quality, so the private confectioner is gaining increasing numbers of customers.*[1]

Here, that is, at the very beginning, I will leave behind forever that apparently innocent time, free of the symbolic, the time when the burek was not yet laden with meanings, encumbered with mythologies, poisoned by ideologies, constructed by discourse.

Today—half a century after the appearance of the news snippet about the first-rate bureks—things are, well, different. You can still, at least in my opinion, get a relatively decent burek. But since the time when it lost its innocence, that "first-rate" burek has entered the hermetic house of Sloveneness, the central Slovene house of culture, the Cankarjev dom Cultural and Congress Centre, and has not remained unnoticed even by such cultural illiterates as nutritionists. Its range and recognition have even spawned ideas such as placing the "pizza burek"—an authentically Slovene product that unites new and old Europe, West and East—on the

---

1 Anon., "Novomeška kronika" [Novo Mesto Chronicle], *Dolenjski list*, September 22, 1966, 13. The burekstatements in this chapter have not been burdened with references. There are two reasons for this. Firstly, I did not wish to burden such an already encumbered text with references. Secondly, all of the burekstatements in this chapter appear in the chapters which follow, in which they are equipped with all of the necessary "scientific" apparatus.

European coat of arms and flag. During this time we have given the burek so many meanings that it often seems as if no one knows what it is anymore. Health food or junk food? Foreign or Slovene? Worthless fast food or trustworthy traditional food? Cool or crap? Slovene food or non-Slovene food? Something to be denied and excluded, or honoured and glorified? Patrician food or plebeian food? Urban cuisine or country pie? "The shit" or just shit? Something to get rid of and forget about, or something to put on the coat of arms and the flag?

Something mysterious, metaphysical even, has found its way into the often trivial, bizarre burek. Spelled backwards it reads *kerub*, the Slovene word for cherub, as many have noted. Of course, you wouldn't get agreement on our mysterious relation to cherubs, either. But who would expect to?

Perhaps it is that unclear entity which hides behind the word *truth*. That uncertain thing which Friedrich Nietzsche so often sought and always answered in the same manner: what is truth, if not illusion?[2] But in this text we will not put truth into words. We will avoid it, reject it, renounce it by turning to less metaphysical absolute truths. Truths about unhealthiness, Balkanness, plebeianism, foreignness and so on which move the burek from the realm of self-evident materiality, a primary need, something to stuff yourself with, into the realm of culture. Truths that unlike common, eternal, unchangeable, self-evident truths, have to constantly struggle for their existence. Truths that can be changed, erased, supplanted by other truths at any moment. Truths that are true mainly through their consequences.

In this analysis therefore, the burek is always the metaburek. It is greasy, Balkan, Slovene, non-Slovene, the greatest, eastern, the best, shit, oriental, unhealthy, plebeian, Yugoslav, junk, a cherub. It is never a completely pure, innocent, unconditioned burek. And it is this more

---

2 This is one of Nietzsche's leitmotifs, which appears quite frequently, of course using different words, in numerous texts. For instance: "Actually, why do we even assume that 'true' and 'false' are intrinsically opposed? Isn't it enough to assume that there are levels of appearance and, as it were, lighter and darker shades and tones of appearance—different *valeurs* [values], to use the language of painters? Why shouldn't the world *that is relevant to us*—be a fiction? And if someone asks: 'But doesn't fiction belong with an author?'—couldn't we shoot back: '*Why?* Doesn't this 'belonging' belong, perhaps, to fiction as well?'" (Friedrich Nietzsche, *Beyond Good and Evil: Prelude to the Philosophy of the Future*, trans. Judith Norman [Cambridge: Cambridge University Press, 2002], 35)

than just a burek—this metaburek,[3] in order to avoid misunderstandings—which is the main and in fact the only subject of my analysis.

The Metaburek and Discourse

The metaburek unfortunately requires some sort of theoretical treatment in order to define it precisely; as such it demands, of course, science.

The first difficulty arises very quickly. The metaburek appears, expresses and manifests itself in very different forms. The cool and crap burek exist in both language and in material practice. We can exalt it and scorn it in both word and action. If we take it a step farther, we notice that the metaburek is found in audio images (e.g. the cult song by Slovene rapper Ali En "Sirni & mesni" [Cheese and meat (burek)] floating in the air), visual images (the same song, listed on the cover of his CD "Leva scena" [The Left(ist) Scene] or a photograph of a burek in Ali En's hands published in *Mladina* magazine), as well as the direct enjoyment of that particular burek, which can also be understood as a sort of physical image (the same burek—and not a Carniolan sausage—in Ali En's hands, thus not in a photograph but standing in front of the burek stand on Miklošičeva street late at night on a gloomy day). So we can talk about spoken (in the above case sung, but it can also be used as a curse, chatted about, theorized about), written, photographed and otherwise visually imaged, nutritional and probably other metabureks. As Roland Barthes would say, they are "different systems, according to which substance is used in communication."[4] Of course, these systems can be defined and broken down differently.

We could talk about systems of objects, images and behaviour. And this trinity can be reduced to a duality or expanded to a higher number of components, in very different ways. For instance, a system of objects

---

3 I shall attempt to maintain the analytical distinction between the "metaburek" and the unconditioned burek. Except in cases where this distinction is excessively blurred or unclear, I will use the analytically foggy concept of "burek."

4 Roland Barthes, *Elements of Semiology*, trans. Annette Lavers and Colin Smith (London: Cape, 1969), 7.

could be understood and classified as a system of practices on one hand and a system of images on the other. We could perform the same reduction with a system of images or practices, or expand them through new divisions.

One can speak of linguistic and non-linguistic semiotic systems. The latter would include bodily or, more clearly, physical systems of representation, such as body language and signals, dance, that which Pierre Bourdieu called "body hexis,"[5] and on the other hand a large number of heterogeneous forms of representation, such as painting, sculpture, photography, music, film and so on. And after all of this organizing we still couldn't say that the analysis is finished, this love of order would not eliminate the need for further study, work which it would seem has no end.

The issue is further complicated when we put individual examples, i.e. manifestations of the metaburek, under the microscope. That is, one manifestation, one text, to use the semiotic term, can combine several semiotic systems. It is, as Adam Jaworski and Nikolas Coupland would say, "multimodal."[6] A hypothetical television advertisement for bureks would probably contain both spoken and written language, still and moving images, live acting and computer-generated images, music and more. But actually we don't have to search for examples in the hypothetical world.

The real world further complicates the issue. In the case of this enticing photograph we are undoubtedly talking about a very complex system in which various substances and various languages are operating or at least present. And very different, complex, and not always clear relationships are formed between them. The basic medium, if we can even speak of a basic medium, through which this manifestation of the metaburek is accessible, is photography. We could therefore speak of the language of photography. Then, intrinsically or extrinsically to that, depending on how we break the image down, there is linguistic language (the word "art," and the word "burek" on the window in the background) and

5 See Pierre Bourdieu, "Language and Symbolic Power," in *The Discourse Reader*, ed. Adam Jaworski, and Nikolas Coupland (London; New York: Routledge, 1999), 502–513.

6 Adam Jaworski and Nikolas Coupland, "Introduction: Perspectives on Discourse Analysis," in *The Discourse Reader*, 7.

Figure 1. The Burek as "ART." Borut Peterlin, in "Piera Ravnikar, programska direktorica" [Piera Ravnikar, Program Director], *Mladina*, September 16, 2006, 63. Courtesy of *Mladina*.

the language of objects (the word "ART" written in burek or using burek-substance and not in greasy red letters in the small print font Lucida Sans Unicode or with a Carniolan sausage, the kebab in the right-hand corner and other objects). These two languages together, the word "art" written in burek, create a new, let's say completely infelicitous, artistic language. And this artistic language is in no way reducible to the language of photography. It is structured differently, it has different rules... But I should end this game of detection and dissection of the multi-substantiality, multimodality, and multi-linguisticity of the metaburek, as it has done its job: it has brought us to the first serious question in this project: is it even possible to include, embrace, think about all of this heterogeneous material with its extremely different forms of expression, these different substances, linguistic systems, this multimodality?

We shall resolve this difficulty using the concept of *discourse*. From the point of view of a particular discourse, for instance the discourse of consuming a burek, the difference between the linguistic act (ordering a burek) and the physical act (eating a burek) is unimportant. Both statements, both linguistic and physical, extralinguistic acts, are discursive—sensible within a certain discourse. As Ernesto Laclau and Chantal Mouffe point out, these actions have something in common which enables their correlation.[7] And this is the fact that both of them comprise the entire procedure—the consumption of a burek. A statement is (or can be) both a linguistic or non-linguistic act, both a practice and a representation of very different phenomenal, substantive forms.

But we still have not entirely answered the question. Let's go back for a moment to the enticing photograph. In the sense of some artistic discourse, some artistic language, the burek is (just) speech or a speech act, to use Ferdinand de Saussure's conceptual dichotomy of language/speech.[8] The burek is therefore just one of the elements within the numerous variations and combinations of artistic language, just one of the elements of a certain syntagm. Of course it could also be the other way around. From the point of view of a particular burekdiscourse, if we can even speak of such a discourse, then the speech act is a specific artistic form. The artistic form is just one of the variations within bureklanguage.

It might not be out of place here to say more about *statements*, the elementary units of discourse. The concept of statement was not selected lightly. It leads us to Foucault's masterpiece, to archaeology, with which, to put it mildly, my humble endeavour has very little in common. Why statement then? The statement—the elementary unit of discourse—has the status of a unique event. A statement, according to Foucault, from whom I have (it must be said) very superficially, freely and probably also heretically borrowed the concept,[9] is "always

---

7 Ernesto Laclau and Chantal Mouffe, "Post-Marxism without Apologies," in *New Reflections on the Revolution of Our Time*, ed. Ernesto Laclau (London; New York: Verso, 1990), 100.

8 Ferdinand de Saussure, *Course on General Linguistics*, trans. and annotated by Roy Harris (New York: Philosophical Library, 1959).

9 Foucault defines the concept of statement very comprehensively in *The Archaeology of Knowledge*. If in my case as I have already mentioned I freely interpret the concept primarily to underscore the uniqueness of the event, the irreducibility of statements, in Foucault's case it is an extensive and quite complex programme which is perhaps best described in this part of the text: "To describe a group of statements not as the closed, plethoric totality of a meaning, but as incomplete, fragmented figure; to describe a group of statements not with reference to the interiority of an intention, a thought, or a subject, but in accordance with the dispersion of an exteriority; to

an event that neither the language *(langue)* nor the meaning can quite exhaust."[10] A statement therefore can never be directly, without residuals, reducible to a signifier and other structuralist categories. This direct reducibility is eliminated precisely by its always also being an event. An event simply means that it occurs. We are speaking of an event that "is neither substance nor accident, neither quality nor process; the event is not of the order of bodies."[11] And although, as Foucault continues, "it is not in any way non-material; it always has effect, the effect is on the material level; it has its place and exists in the relation, coexistence, diffusion, division, accumulation, and selection of material elements; it is not an action or a property of a body."[12]

Events and statements thus proceed with a certain kind of regularity, and create threads that become entwined in certain types of repetition, remain and at the same time are changed through repetition, form networks, etc. A statement is certainly a strange event, "because, like every event, it is unique, yet subject to repetition, transformation, and reactivation."[13] It is also a strange event "because it is linked not only to the situations that provoke it, and to the consequences that it gives rise to, but at the same time, and in accordance with a quite different modality, to the statements that precede and follow it."[14]

Let's look at two completely different examples of the referentiality of statements. We'll start with the aphorism "We love Jurek more than burek," with which Slovenes (using Serbo-Croatian) marked Slovene skier Jure Franko's silver medal at the Olympic Games in Sarajevo in 1984

---

describe a group of statements, in order to rediscover not the moment or the trace of their origin, but the specific forms of an accumulation, is certainly not to uncover an interpretation, to discover a foundation, or to free constituent acts; nor is it to decide on a rationality, or to embrace a teleology. It is to establish what I am quite willing to call a *positivity.*" (Foucault, *The Archaeology of Knowledge*, 141) My use of Foucault's concept differs not only in its intent, but also with regard to various "technical" specificities. To illustrate I shall mention just one, probably the most visible. In *The Archaeology of Knowledge*, on page 31, Foucault limits a statement to "the gesture of writing or to the articulation of speech," but he goes on to say that "on the other hand it also opens up to itself a residual existence in the field of a memory, or in the materiality of manuscripts, books, or any other form of recording." My concept of a statement is, let's say, less exclusive.

10 Foucault, *The Archaeology of Knowledge*, 31.

11 Michel Foucault, "The Order of Discourse," in *Untying the Text: A Post-Structuralist Reader*, ed. Robert Young (Boston: Routledge; Kegan Paul, 1981), 69.

12 Ibid.

13 Foucault, *The Archaeology of Knowledge*, 31.

14 Ibid.

(Yugoslavia's first medal at a Winter Olympic Games), and then add the phraseme "You're a burek" which is frequently used in Slovene slang to denote incompetents, fools, and other similar creatures. In 1999, in an entertainment supplement to a Slovene daily, Slovene Alpine Skiing team coach Tone Vogrinec, responding to criticisms of the lack of success of the national team in Vail, concluded with a highly original declaration of his attitude towards champion skier Jure Košir (in fact these are not his words, but those of the writer of the article, a professional troublemaker): "I admit that I love Jurek more than burek. Anyone who thinks Jurek is a burek, is a burek." And another example of the referentiality of statements: the reduction and use of healthier fats in bureks by the Dino fast food chain, a statement that was preceded and followed by other similar statements. Before they did this it had been done, of course not in an identical manner, by the Pečjak Bakery and many other burekproducers, and many others have done it in different ways since.

Every statement is therefore at the same time both unique and referential. This implies that the repetition carries the same weight as the original. The great names and events in the history of the burek, at least at this first level of analysis, have to be treated without privilege, equal to all the others. This indifference to station or levelling of statements also constitutes a lack of concern for the traditional hierarchy of disciplines. Appearing at the same level in the set of statements are popular music written in honour of the burek; serious nutritional science, which more touches on the burek rather than giving it serious treatment; science-fiction, which uses it to enrich its stories; producing and selling bureks, which are not sets which are independent of discourse; and high-school slang, which would be much poorer without the burek. But as Foucault says, "it's not a matter of locating everything on one level, that of the event, but of realizing that there are actually a whole order of levels of different types of events differing in amplitude, chronological breadth, and capacity to produce effects."[15]

Through listing these examples we touch on something else. The metaburek thus manifests in some kind of burekstatements. But what

15 Michel Foucault, "Truth and Power," in *Power/Knowledge: Selected Interviews and Other Writings, 1972–1977*, ed. Colin Gordon (New York: Pantheon Books, 1980), 114.

is a burekstatement? A burekstatement is a statement that includes a burek from various substantive systems. But a distinction quickly arises between them. On one hand we have statements in which the burek is (merely) a signifier of something else, i.e. stands for something else. For instance in the phraseme "to be a burek" it signifies, i.e. connotes, a feeble, mentally challenged being, an incompetent. We could call these indirect burekstatements, i.e. statements in which the burek clearly signifies something, unproblematically and generously lending its name to ideas, concepts, thoughts, etc. On the other hand we have statements that refer to the burek more directly. These are statements in which the burek does not signify—at least not clearly—anything but itself. An example of a direct burekstatement? How about Ali En's rap song "Sirni & mesni" [Cheese and meat (burek)]:

> *Burek (8 x)*
> *I got a friend, his name is Frank, to eat a burek he robbed a bank,*
> *But hey Frank, how does that help you, in prison you get dry bread and mouldy stew.*
> *What'cha gonna do when the burek is gone, the cold is sticking to your bones,*
> *Think about it, use your head, get out quick and grab that bread.*
> *Burek (8 x)*
> *Burek, burek, it keeps your belly from cold and strife,*
> *And sometimes you need strength to protect your wife.*
> *When the postman turned away from our door, he saw our neighbour and said what the hell,*
> *These guys are strong, these guys are wild, they don't eat no other food but meaty cheesy burek*
> *Burek (8 x)*

Of course this division into indirect and direct burekstatements is problematic for several reasons. Even a so-called direct burekstatement signifies, or more precisely connotes, something else. In Ali En's hit, the burek connotes something cool, alright, filling, powerful and probably even healthy. Semanticizing thus seems to be unavoidable. For

Figure 2. "I don't have [enough] for a burek." Photo by Toni Dugorepec, in Jure Aleksič, "Rdeči November" [Red November], *Mladina*, November 23, 2007, 46.

instance, according to Barthes, "as soon as there is a society, every usage is converted into a sign of itself".[16] Thus the purpose of a burek is to fill your stomach, and that purpose cannot be separated from a sign for food (which is most clearly expressed in the phraseme "you don't have [enough money] for a burek," which is a substitute or complementary version of the phraseme "you don't have [enough money] for bread."

As seen in Figure 2, a protester holds a sign that reads "I don't have [enough] for a burek." And we could of course go on and on. A burek is intended to fill your belly in a hurry, and this purpose cannot be separated from a sign for fast food. A burek is intended to fill your belly when everything else is closed, and this purpose cannot be separated from a sign for food for night-owls, etc.

Such a division is also problematic because the line between direct and indirect statements is often hard to determine. For instance in the example of the photo of the burek shaped to form the word "ART" we can't actually say whether it is a direct or indirect statement, or we can

16 Barthes, *Elements of Semiology*, 12.

say that it is both. It depends on the language, the substance which we put under the burekological microscope.

Thus we use statements, units of discourse that have substance, support, place and date, to indicate the presence of discourse in an event. A statement is therefore a discursive event. As Foucault says, "we must be ready to receive every moment of discourse in its sudden irruption."[17]

But we also have to understand that statement-making is only one of the formulations present in discourse. Discourse, as Foucault says, is a sum of hypotheses, a sum of ethical choices, institutional rules, models of learning, etc., as well as a sum of statements, i.e. discursive events.[18] Thus it is clearly insufficient, if not actually wrong, to define discourse solely on the basis of a codified system of statement-making. A statement "is not an ideal form that can be actualized in any body, at any time, in any circumstances, and in any material conditions."[19] A statement therefore appears, is articulated and corrected within objective parameters. It is not therefore a manifestation of discourses that are independent of the objective world, but a discursive manifestation adjusted to an objective, non-discursive field.

Our analysis of the metaburek thus poses the question of the relationship of statements to the non-discursive, and raises the issue of the understanding and analysis of practices, representations and objects that are not completely comprehensible through the analysis of statements. But at this point in the analysis it is particularly important to recognize the existence of the discursive in statements, regardless of how and how much some statement is subordinate to any non-discursive, objective space. We should perhaps approach this under a different title.

The Metaburek and the (Non-)Discursive

Such a tactic—surrendering the metaburek to the fearsome autonomy of discourse—also leads us to an unpleasant question: What does the

17 Foucault, *The Archaeology of Knowledge*, 28.
18 Ibid, 37.
19 Ibid, 117.

metaburek have in common with the burek? The pristine, uncorrupted, unconditioned burek, which exists independently of the metaburek?

Discourses produce their own discursive objects, which never coincide with unconditioned objects. A burekstatement is not the same thing as an unconditioned burek and is also not just an extension of it. The graffito "Burek? Nein danke" (a popular meme which appeared during Slovenia's rise to independence) is not the same as the unconditioned burek which is being baked and sold just a few streets away by an Albanian from Macedonia. From this perspective, the statement and the unconditioned burek are radically heterogeneous; an impassable rift appears between the discursive and the non-discursive.

But at the same time the discursive and the non-discursive are continuously intertwined, if we choose to see them that way. Thus nationalist discourse can appear once as a linguistic representation on a city wall (for instance the graffito "Burek? Nein danke"), and again as an element in the justification of the institutional practice of excluding the burek (for instance the argument by an event organizer that French canapés should be served instead of bureks), or as a (re)interpretation of these practices (for instance, when the burek surprisingly and unexpectedly shows up at a formal event at Cankarjev dom, Slovenia's central cultural institution, and elicits similar and other responses). Therefore between discursive and non-discursive elements there is "a sort of interplay of shifts of positions and modifications of function which can also vary very widely."[20] In other words, the production of discourse is unavoidably founded on institutional and other non-discursive, objective bases. It is introduced and reinforced by a whole system of activities, practices, fields, institutions, etc. (education, production, consumption, legislation), which are activated, understood, and reflected differently in different situations.

Following Foucault, we shall call this set of discursive and non-discursive elements an apparatus (*dispositif*).[21] I thus wish to define, using

20 Michel Foucault, "The Confession of the Flesh," in *Power/Knowledge*, 195.

21 Foucault first used the concept of the apparatus in his book *Discipline and Punish: The Birth of the Prison* (trans. Alan Sheridan [New York: Pantheon Books, 1977]), in which, however, he did not give explicit definitions of the concept. On one hand he isolated the enunciative field, which determines the legal definition of delinquency, defines new types of social welfare, etc., and on the

the concept of the apparatus, the nature of the connections that exist between these heterogeneous, discursive and non-discursive elements. In other words, I also want to define, describe, and embrace an objective field which permits the production of statements—the operation of the discursive.

But even with this we have still not answered the question posed above. What does the metaburek have in common with the unconditioned burek? In the burekapparatus we find a lot—in my analysis an appalling majority—of situations, events and statements in which no trace of the unconditioned burek can be found.

In order to tease out the concept of the unconditioned burek we must include the dimension of genesis within the concept of the apparatus. The apparatus, according to Foucault, is "a perpetual process of strategic elaboration."[22] I would rather speak of a process of discursive elaboration, or discursive augmentation. Discursive elaboration in which a 0 point appears, some (pre)discursive condition of the burekapparatus, some not yet discursive burekapparatus, which enables or establishes the burekapparatus. We can find this in the intentionally anonymous statement at the beginning of this chapter, but in order to save the reader the trouble of turning the pages, we'll repeat it.

In the rhythm of urban life the burek stands of foreign burek producers and sellers were places where people could quickly ease their hunger pangs, supplement their lunches, or make up for a long absence from home with an unconditioned burek. This was done by certain groups of people, primarily those who did not have ready access to a home-cooked meal: secondary-school and college students, immigrants, workers, travellers and visitors, people in transit, people in a hurry. (In this paragraph the past tense perhaps does not exclude other tenses, since all of the above also applies to the present.)

---

other hand prison and other institutions of control and punishment with a specific organization of space, objects and visibility. But an institution, as Foucault emphasizes, is not a product of legal and other discourses. A delinquent, as defined in legal discourse, is not the same person as a criminal in prison. The concept of apparatus is defined more explicitly (although this adverb does not seem to be the best-suited to Foucault's descriptions of theoretical/analytical concepts) in "The Confession of the Flesh", an interview conducted by Alain Grosrichard.

22 Foucault, "The Confession of the Flesh," 195.

At this zero point, in this situation that establishes the burekapparatus, we are dealing with the unconditioned burek and the material practice associated with it, the so-called primary need, i.e. eating! This is historically and geographically determined and thus set in the rhythm of everyday life and individual and social reproduction.

The other types of practice that include the burek are discursive, labelled with meaning through this fundamental practice, and thus explainable in relation to it and with reference to it, but of course not always directly. Why did the graffito "Burek? Nein danke" even appear? Why would any nationalistic discourse bite into the unconditioned burek? Because the production and sale of the unconditioned burek is (was) in the suspect hands of immigrants, more precisely Albanians from Macedonia. And why did the burek become greasy junk food? Why was the dietetic, healthy lifestyle discourse of the unconditioned burek pulled out of the realm of primary need into the realm of the greasy and unhealthy? Because it was a very or perhaps even the most widespread, the most visible and most accessible fast food, whose production was among other things, as stated, in the suspect hands of immigrants, less subject to the dietetic Big Brother. Okay, that's enough for now. Let's leave something for the following chapters.

The apparatus is therefore defined by some structure of heterogeneous elements, as well as by a certain type of genesis, or elaboration. In other words, the metaburek is a genesis, a formation, it has a history. And in this genesis we cannot overlook the place of the unconditioned burek. To put it simply and banally, without the unconditioned burek there is no metaburek.

But what actually is the burekapparatus? We could describe it as the sum or the genesis of various situations that enable the burek to be associated with various discourses and thus generates the metaburek, which is manifested in statements. Such situations could be associated with eating, making or buying bureks, and can include talking about, writing about, photographing or depicting bureks, or some entirely different activity which to some extent draws in, includes or touches on bureks. It can also relate to more covert practices, such as certain forms of regulating consumption which directly or indirectly concern bureks, or completely invisible practices, such as exclusion, tabooization, covering up or eliminating bureks or some other reality associated with them in one way or another.

We therefore find the burekapparatus in very different places. It skulks and swaggers about in kitchens, in the media, on the street, among immigrants and natives, in schools, in pop culture, among youth, in conscious or unconscious speech, in subcultures, in physical and symbolic space, in science, in tradition, on walls and on paper, in scientific and lay texts, among liberals and conservatives, in fiction and non-fiction, in sound and solid media, among aficionados and disparagers, among you and us.

The burekapparatus is therefore a place where the objective, historical and discursive meet, a place which within the framework of objective, historical possibilities produces statements and activates discourse. In short, it generates the metaburek.

Of course, we might ask how reasonable and necessary it is to differentiate the discursive and the non-discursive or extra-discursive. The division into discursive and extra-discursive, according to Laclau and Mouffe, means an acceptance of the classical division into an objective field, constituted without a discursive element, and discourse as a pure reflection of thought. But the more we analyze so-called non-discursive complexes (political interventions, technology, manufacturing organizations) the clearer it becomes that these are not systems conditioned by an objective force (God, Nature, Fate) and therefore have to be understood, say the authors in question, as discursive articulations.[23]

It is not difficult to agree with this. Discourses, probably most visibly through institutions (regulations, laws), clearly project into non-discursive spaces and regulate them. For instance, this is how healthy-lifestyle discourse affected the reduction of fat in the production and substance of bureks. The production of bureks is thus in no way a complex independent of discourse. But this does not mean that we have to reject the analytic distinction between discursive and non-discursive. Discourse in this case is primarily or solely an analytical tool and not a

23 Ernesto Laclau and Chantal Mouffe, *Hegemony and Socialist Strategy: Towards a Radical Democratic Politics* (London; New York: Verso, 2001), 90–91.

hallowed theoretical concept which we would want to raise to the level of an absolute.[24]

To return for a moment to the initial question of this section, we can add that the concept of an apparatus makes a case for and substantiates our analysis. It gives us a viewpoint focused on the exclusivity and uniqueness of an object, in our case, the burek. Without drawing the objective field into analysis, such a tactic—based on the uniqueness of an object—would seem strange, deficient or even wrong. Without the field of the objective—therefore in the totalitarian regime of discourse—we would probably have to choose a discursive uniqueness as our starting point, and not the uniqueness of the object. In the dictatorship of discourse the concept of the uniqueness of the object could cost us our head.

To conclude, the metaburek, at least in this analysis, is not constituted only by the weight of some vehement, self-absorbed and fearsome discourses, but also in the non-discursive, objective field, in the framework of objective possibility. The metaburek is always associated with the unconditioned burek, although it sometimes seems as if the distance between the two could be measured in light years.

The Metaburek and the (Im)Material

The undogmatic concept of the apparatus indicates something further. Unlike general theories, it proposes or even demands that we should begin with an analysis of the substance, and not from relatively a priori concepts, to which the substance—whatever it may be—is added only by way of illustration.

But what in fact is the substance in our case? Substance in its most primary, grounded, material sense? Actually, the question of materiality

24 Because of this avoidance of a clear definition of discourse, we also will not say that there is a dialectical process between discursive and non-discursive fields (institutions, practices, social structures and everything that we in fact place in the objective field), that discourse is also formed using non-discursive elements, and at the same time also has a reverse effect on these non-discursive elements. This would actually be the easiest way to alleviate the dualism, but at the same time it would strike deeply into the definition of discourse itself. This is in no way my wish or intention.

would be more reasonably approached using a different, better-considered tactic and not through this odd wordplay. That is, if we include the field of objective possibilities in our analysis, then we quickly find ourselves faced with the problem of the materiality of the object of study. Adding objective possibilities to our analysis of the metaburek also presents the question of materiality and the functional context of that materiality.

Here it would first of all seem reasonable to define the distinction between the materiality of the unconditioned burek and that of the metaburek.

Let's begin with the metaburek. The materiality of the metaburek? The metaburek is not in the realm of the material, it does not belong to the world of physical bodies, but in the realm of the universal, the world of ideas, meanings, thoughts, opinions, conceptions, theories. This of course does not mean that it is not embodied in sensible elements. It manifests in statements, as we have already noted. In order to treat a sequence of linguistic or non-linguistic elements as a statement, it needs to have material existence, or better, a material backing. A statement, according to Foucault, "is always given through some material medium, even if that medium is concealed, even if it is doomed to vanish as soon as it appears."[25]

Of course statements about materiality have very different characteristics, and very different lifetimes, which can last for millennia (for instance the graffito "Burek? Nein danke," which archaeologists will uncover in a millennium or two when digging the foundations for a new national library) or just a few seconds, or less than a second (for instance the well-known phraseme "to be a burek" or the leading Slovene nationalist Zmago Jelinčič Esq. biting into a burek). In all of these examples it was actually stated, in one way or another materialized, and did not remain only in the sphere of ideas, thoughts, meanings, and conceptions. A statement is not, as we have said, "an ideal form that can be actualized in any body, at any time, in any circumstances, and in any material conditions."[26]

25 Foucault, *The Archaeology of Knowledge*, 112.
26 Ibid, 117.

However, in this section what we are actually interested in is the materiality of the unconditioned burek. Unlike the metaburek, excuse me, unlike the materially conditioned manifestations of the metaburek, it is much more self-evident. But precisely owing to this self-evidence, this unconditionedness, it presents a unique analytic and theoretical problem.

According to Daniel Miller, objects exist as physical, concrete forms, and at that level they are independent of any mental representations of them. In short, the unconditioned burek exists independently of the metaburek. This quality is a crucial element to understanding the power and significance of objects in cultural formation. The reality, the physicality of material culture is not just a bridge or a bond between the mental and physical worlds, but also between the conscious and unconscious. Physicality, as Miller states, makes objects real and obvious but also causes them to be included in unconscious, unreflected behaviour.[27]

Objects are not words, and when we speak about the meaning of words, says Miller, the main emphasis is more connected "with questions of 'being' rather than questions of 'reference.'"[28] In comparison with language, the physicality of artefacts is much more difficult to separate from the social context in which they function, and therefore they also cause a unique academic problem.

This is very freely put. However, in the conceptual framework of Miller's central thoughts about material culture, this is not only the setting for social action, but an integral part of social action. It puts material culture in a processual and relational position with respect to subjects. It puts it in a position in which objects and their ability to form things support the development of the subject.[29] Material culture is

27 Daniel Miller, *Material Culture and Mass Consumption* (Oxford; New York: Blackwell, 1987), 99.

28 Daniel Miller, "Artefacts and the Meaning of Things," in *Companion Encyclopedia of Anthropology*, ed. Tim Ingold (London; New York: Routledge, 1994), 397.

29 The key word and idea of Miller's monumental work *Material Culture and Mass Consumption* is "objectification," and it is used to describe a series of processes in which objects are shown as constitutive elements in the formation of the subject. Objectification determines a type of dialectic relationship between subjects and objects, between people and things, and does not privilege the limits of personality, as they are understood in "the west": "Objectification describes the inevitable process by which all expression, conscious or unconscious, social or individual, takes specific form. It is only through the giving of form that something can be conceived of. The term objectification, however, always implies that form is a part of a larger process of becoming." (Miller, *Material Culture*, 81).

therefore culture, culture in the broadest sense, it is a process through which communities and individuals are socialized, establish themselves, and constitute themselves.

But the materiality of the unconditioned burek does not end at this general level of materiality. In the case of the unconditioned burek (and in certain manifestations of the metaburek) we have to deal with a special type of material culture, "embodied material culture," a special class of material objects made to be immediately destroyed.[30] Destroyed through eating, through the introduction of food into the human body. Owing to its close connection to the body, this specific material culture has additional symbolic and emotional significance in the formation of personality. It is therefore also a material construction of personality, and not only in the figurative sense. In view of the fact that eating and drinking are acts that have to be repeated every day for biological survival, they occupy a very important place among the numerous routine practices that, as Pierre Bourdieu reminds us, serve to consolidate habitus—the system of bodily dispositions that structure our actions and unconsciously instil social roles and cultural categories, perceptions, identities and differentiation.[31]

And this is not yet the full range of this embodied material culture. Since the maintenance of these processes of consumption also requires the constant maintenance of production via manufacturing, cooking and other work, the close and deep-seated dialectical relationship

---

This value of material culture as a form of "living in the world" is probably most evident in his understanding of socialization. Later in his theoretical analysis, using the example of psychological and psychoanalytical studies he clearly demonstrates the importance of objects to the development of the subject. These studies show that only through a truly dynamic relationship between an infant and his environment is a subject capable of becoming a subject. As Miller forcefully emphasizes elsewhere, a child born in a particular cultural environment very quickly develops noticeably different behaviours from a child raised in a different environment. The microroutines of everyday life have a major impact on this. They guide us in our interactions with our environment, with objects and with the tiny but significant differences in the forms of the objects through which we form our classifications and habitus. This therefore allows a large part of the world to become quickly absorbed in what seems to be the self-evident context of our lives. In this sense our cultural identity is not only embodied, but also objectified and materialized. (Miller, "Artefacts and the Meaning of Things," 399)

30 See Michael Dietler, "Introduction: Embodied Material Culture," *Archaeological Review from Cambridge* 20 (2005): 3–5.

31 See Pierre Bourdieu, *Practical Reason: On the theory of Action*, trans. Randal Johnson (Stanford: Stanford University Press, 1998).

between domestic and political economy is particularly visible in the realm of material culture. The consumption of embodied material culture forms the basic domain for negotiations, projections and constellations of power. Embodied material culture is thus a good example of what Marcel Mauss called "total social phenomena."[32]

But what does the materiality of the unconditioned burek (if it is so embodied) have to do with the metaburek? We shall answer this question with a question, but before we get to this question-answer we have to make a few assertions. It is not unimportant which kind of materiality and/or functional context appears in the realm of the discursive. And before that we would have to say that it is especially important what types of objects—material or non-material—appear in the realm of the discursive. To put it differently, the types of objects, or materiality if there is any, which have to be dealt with, matter to discourse. It matters to the metaburek that the unconditioned burek is something that fills your belly. And that it is a belly-filler with a very specific place in the order of belly-fillers. So we can ask ourselves why for instance did nationalistic discourse take the burek closer to heart than e.g. čevapčiči (referred to as "weenies" for a brief time after Slovenia's independence) or the legendary Yugo (one of the most popular Yugoslav cars of the 80s, also an export item and the butt of numerous jokes)? We can supplement the question through guesswork. If an expression for a recognized object was chosen from the language of the former federal republic, for instance the pointed-toed shoes called špičaki, once very popular among immigrants and often a source of amusement to Slovenes, the analysis probably would not be repeated following the same coordinates; various new discourses would enter the story, old discourses would find a new place and meaning and a lot of other things might surprise us.

Let's be clear that we shall not be overly burdened by these kinds of questions and guesswork in this project. However, despite the

32 See Marcel Mauss, *The Gift: The forms and Functions of Exchange in Archaic Societies*, trans. Ian Cunnison (London: Cohen and West Ltd., 1954). In these "total social phenomena," as Mauss calls them, "all kinds of institutions find simultaneous expression: religious, legal, moral, and economic. In addition, the phenomena have their aesthetic aspect and they reveal morphological types." (Mauss, *The Gift*, 1)

apparent lack of importance of materiality to understanding the metaburek, it is not or may not be neglected, at least in our analysis. In other words, it matters to the metaburek whether a transport vehicle, a linguistic form or a belly-filler is hiding behind the unconditioned burek. And to take it further, what kind of belly-filler it is also matters to the metaburek. Is it a belly-filler intended for all bellies, which some might avoid for instance because of its low price, or a belly-filler for people who solve their emotional problems by buying BMWs or gold-plated golf clubs?

In this analysis of the metaburek, the material features and range of the unconditioned burek will also have a significant emphasis. We will not overlook or remain silent about the fact that the burek is also food, a belly-filler, and not just a symbolic medium, a tool in signification processes. And not just an important food for certain ethnic, peer, etc. groups, but also a food which due to its popularity and visibility in the urban street milieu is also a signifier of fast food. A food which has guaranteed itself a place in the group of winners in the Slovenian late modern, both in terms of quantitative growth and in terms of expansion into numerous new domains and institutions (for instance industrial production, consumption in schools, the military, at numerous formal and informal parties and events). It is therefore a food with all the material, functional and other contextual manifestations which a focus on the currently fashionable discursive might quickly overlook.

But lest we forget, the subject of our analysis is the metaburek.

The Metaburek and Discourse (Part II)

Let us therefore return to discourses, the forces which destroy the evidentness of materiality, and look at the metaburek more closely through a discursive, idealistic perspective.

Discourse, according to Laclau and Mouffe, tells us that every social configuration is meaningful.[33] If a burek is eaten by leading Slovene

33 Laclau and Mouffe, "Post-Marxism Without Apologies," 101.

nationalist Zmago Jelinčič Esq. or by an immigrant from Bosnia, the physical act, the material practice is the same, but its meaning is different. But this example is perhaps not the best; let's find another. The same object, a cheese burek, is often referred to in Slovene professional and popular texts about healthy lifestyles as "greasy junk food," while among immigrants from Bosnia and Herzegovina in Slovenia it's not even a burek, but a "sirnica" (sir = cheese). Furthermore, and this is essential to our project, for them it is nearly a holy object, as Bosnian pop musician Dino Merlin has explained in numerous interviews: he called his 2004 album Burek (and not Sirnica). The same object thus has different meanings within different discourses—i.e. within the healthy lifestyle and immigrant-ethnic discourses. Of course the burek as an object (the unconditioned burek) exists independently of discursive articulation. Its existence in this analysis is not questioned. But it exists as greasy junk food and as a holy object only within and/or because of various discourses. Or as Laclau and Mouffe put it: "What is denied is not that such objects exist externally to thought, but the rather different assertion that they could constitute themselves as objects outside any discursive condition of emergence."[34] If we therefore pull on the thread from the preceding chapter, we can say that we do not live simply between objects and actions, but between objects and actions which have meanings.

Based on what we have stated in this section we have come close to the meanings. But discourses cannot be understood simply as chains of signifiers or mechanisms of signification. Discourses are of course composed of signs, "but what they do is more than use these signs to designate things."[35] Discourses have to be understood as "practices that systematically form the objects of which they speak."[36] We could also restate, or actually simplify, Foucault's understanding of the constitutive roles of discourses, by saying that the formation of meanings is also or primarily an act of constitution. At any rate, the essential point for the analysis of the metaburek is that we recognize the constitutive

34 Laclau and Mouffe, *Hegemony and Socialist Strategy*, 108.
35 Foucault, *The Archaeology of Knowledge*, 54.
36 Ibid.

role of discourses and meanings.[37] Things therefore obtain meanings and become objects of knowledge only within discourse. The burek as greasy junk food exists only within healthy lifestyle discourse, a discourse which tells us what is healthy and what is unhealthy, a discourse which tells us how to handle greasy, high-calorie food. From a strictly discursive perspective therefore, nothing has meaning outside of discourse. Discourse, according to Foucault, must be conceived "as a violence which we do to things."[38]

The discourses we are speaking about thus do not reflect some "natural" essence of things, but simply *construct* them. Things however are actually always accessible to us through various discourses. These discourses form things and translate them into meaningful units. This constructivist, antiessentialist hypothesis requires that we understand the metaburek, as everyone already knows, as a construct.[39]

This discursive conceptualization of the metaburek is contrary to the idea of the subject as an autonomic creator, an authentic source of meaning (and action). Knowledge or meanings form discourse, and not the subjects which operate within the discourse. As Heidegger said, we don't speak language; language speaks us. From this perspective, the subject is formed within discourse, it is subordinated to its rules, and is therefore dependent upon discourse. The subject is therefore always, like the object,

---

37 We shall restrict ourselves to just one of Foucault's analyses of the objects of knowledge which reveal the constitutive role of discourses. What we refer to today as homosexual behaviour has probably existed from time immemorial. But the category of homosexual as a special form of sexual identity or social subject appeared, as Foucault pointed out in *The History of Sexuality* (trans. Robert Hurley [New York: Vintage Books, 1990]) only within medical, psychiatric, legal and moral discourse in the late 19th century, with the appearance of theories of sexual perversion. Outside of specific discourses, thus outside of the formation of certain behaviours, outside of certain discursive practices, regulations, disciplinary techniques (of particular societies and particular times) the homosexual could not appear as a specific type of social subject. Thus the objects of knowledge, as Foucault showed in the examples of insanity, punishment, crime, disease, homosexuality, etc., exist only within certain discursive formations. From here it is not far to Foucault's understanding or, better, analysis of history. In opposition to historical continuity, at least in the subjects he studied, he inserted fissures, ruptures, discontinuities from period to period, from one discursive formation to the next.

38 Foucault, "The Order of Discourse," 67.

39 I could also define my approach, at least on the basis of what has been said in this section, as a critical discourse analysis. This, as Theo Van Leeuwen says, should be concerned with discourse as the instrument of the social construction of reality (see Theo Van Leeuwen, *Discourse and Practice: New Tools for Critical Discourse Analysis* [Oxford, New York: Oxford University, 2008]). However, there is still a "but." But this will be discussed below.

a discursive subject. Put slightly differently, discourses form only those subject positions through which they become reasonable and effective.

But this does not mean that the subject has to be removed from the analysis of the metaburek. Subjects can, at least it seems so in the case of the metaburek, produce a certain meaning, but that meaning is always formed within rules, in relation to some discourse, some kind of truth. Therefore within discourse we can create or form meanings in different directions. We can bake a "low-fat cheese burek" and not even put it in our mouth, or eat the greasiest burek and make jokes at the expense of patronizing healthy lifestyle discourse. We are thus not (necessarily) passive elements or even products of discursive production. Within discourses, or at least within some discourses, we are given consciousness and creativity. This of course does not mean that all individuals in a certain period will become the subjects of a certain discourse and thus become the objects of its knowledge.

If we therefore adapt and soften the above structuralist motto for the purposes of the analysis of the metaburek, we can most accurately articulate the subject's signifying power by paraphrasing a famous saying from Karl Marx: "People give things meanings, but not in circumstances chosen by themselves."[40]

Thus, to a certain extent I am trying to understand the metaburek as a dynamic exchange between individual authors and individual discourses. Everyone who writes, thinks, talks, sings about, takes photographs of and represents bureks has to take a certain position vis-à-vis the burek. Every subject which makes a statement about a burek does so in a unique and singular manner. None of this occurs in the abstract. Each statement refers and invokes a certain, antecedent discourse, a certain regime of self-evidence, knowledge, and truth. And in addition, each statement about a burek connects to other statements, audiences, institutions, and of course the metaburek itself.

---

40 In the original: "Men make their own history, but they do not make it just as they please; they do not make it under circumstances chosen by themselves..." To which we should add the continuation of these monumental and vividly formulated thoughts: "...but under circumstances directly encountered, given, and transmitted from the past. The tradition of all the dead generations weighs like a nightmare on the brain of the living." (Karl Marx, *The Eighteenth Brumaire of Louis Bonaparte* [Moscow: Progress Publishers, 1967], 10.)

When we speak of the production of meanings within discourse, the meaning of the actions of the subject can be further elucidated by addressing the difference between semantics, which deals with the meaning of words, and pragmatics, which deals with how words are used within certain speech contexts. The question therefore is, to what extent is the rigid separation between semantics and pragmatics, between meaning and usage, reasonable? Usage thus determines meaning and vice versa; usage and meaning are thus inseparably connected. As the wholly committed to "semantics" Ferdinand de Saussure maintained, language is impossible without speech and vice versa.[41]

The Metaburek and Discourse (Part III)

We have therefore left discourse, the central force of the construction of the metaburek, to this complex business of signifying. But signifying, as Humpty Dumpty wisely teaches Alice in Wonderland, is never a neutral act.

> *'When I use a word,' Humpty Dumpty said in rather a scornful tone, 'it means just what I choose it to mean—neither more nor less.'*
> *'The question is,' said Alice, 'whether you can make words mean different things.'*

41 Just a few such thoughts from Saussure: "[L]anguage is necessary if speaking is to be intelligible and produce all its effects; but speaking is necessary for the establishment of language"; "Language and speaking are then interdependent; the former is both the instrument and the product of the latter." (Saussure, *Course in General Linguistics*, 18) Of course, Saussure's language/speech dichotomy is not (entirely) comparable and analogous to that of semantics/pragmatics. The separation between meaning and use has undoubtedly become increasingly blurred from Wittgenstein on. This unblurrable partnership of meaning and use is in fact what Wittgenstein's "talking lion" is telling us: "If a lion could talk, we could not understand him." Why not? The creator of the "talking lion" responds: "[...] when we come into a strange country with entirely strange traditions; and, what is more, even given a mastery of the country's language. We do not *understand* the people. (And not because of not knowing what they are saying to themselves.) We cannot find our feet with them." (Ludwig Wittgenstein, *Philosophical Investigations*, trans. Gertrude Elizabeth Margaret Anscombe [Oxford: Basil Blackwell, 1958], 223e.) The semantic level alone (understanding the meaning of words) is therefore not sufficient to understand language, we also need the pragmatic level (understanding how words are used).

> *'The question is,' said Humpty Dumpty, 'which is to be master—that's all.'*[42]

Meanings and discourses are therefore, as Humpty Dumpty clearly explains, intimately and inseparably associated with power. But, as Foucault says, "discourse is not simply that which translates struggles or systems of domination, but is the thing for which and by which there is struggle, discourse is the power which is to be seized."[43] It is therefore directly both a place and a mechanism of power.

At the level of internal organization, the functioning of discourse first appears as a system of separation. The numerous procedures of separation include prohibition, limitation, differentiation and exclusion, which refer to both object and the manner and conditions of speech and communication, and of course the subjects which are responsible for them.

As Mladen Dolar states, we have to understand discourses "as something internally fractured" and constantly observe what they are forced to eliminate or reject in order to establish themselves.[44] Understanding discourses also requires the invoking of non-events, thus not just an analysis of what is said, but also an analysis of what is not said, or as Dolar says, "not just measuring the weight of the statements, but the weight of the silence."[45] For instance, a glance at Slovene cookbooks reveals a heavy silence and strict discourses that do not allow cookbooks connected in any way with things Slovene to mention bureks.

Exclusion is not the only thing that discourses do. With respect to this analysis it is probably the most problematic and at the same time the most obvious thing that discourses do, and directly implies that discourses cannot be understood without an analysis of power. Discourse, according to Foucault, "appears to be of little account, because the

---

42 Lewis Carroll, *Alice's Adventures in Wonderland and through the Looking-Glass* (Twickenham: Tiger, 1993), 151.

43 Michel Foucault, "The Order of Discourse," 52–53.

44 Mladen Dolar, "Spremna beseda" [Foreword], in *Vednost—oblast—subjekt* [Knowledge—Power—Subject], by Michel Foucault (Ljubljana: Krt, 1991), xvi.

45 Dolar, "Spremna beseda," xvii.

prohibitions that surround it very soon reveal its link with desire and with power."[46]

The metaburek thus has to be understood as formed by all of the statements that have mentioned, described, classified, judged or connected it with other objects. And also—although much more difficult to define—by the statements that have not done so, but which could be expected to, and by all of the unstated statements, the silences which in one way or another surround the burek.

We have said that discourses have a unique power to define and to constitute the objects of knowledge. And we have said that they have the sinister power to erase and exclude. Discourses expand, introduce, reinforce and establish certain meanings and at the same time reject, silence, and erase other meanings, knowledge and truths. We are subordinated to the establishing of truth—in our case it would probably be more appropriate to speak of establishing the self-evident—through power. Power can therefore not be exercised without the production of truth, the self-evident, knowledge.

Truth, knowledge and the self-evident thus cannot exist outside of power. As Foucault said, every society "has its regime of truth, its 'general politics' of truth: that is, the types of discourse which it accepts and makes function as true."[47] Healthy lifestyle discourse, dedicated to the philosophy of healthy living, reinforces certain knowledge, truth, and self-evidence: the burek is an unhealthy thing, greasy junk food. And not only this, it also suggests and often imposes approaches to dealing with greasy junk food, delimits and stigmatizes it.

As stated at the beginning of this chapter, my project is not about relinquishing truth to power and thus setting it against error, alienated consciousness, illusion or ideology.[48] And I am also not trying to draw a

46 Foucault, "The Order of Discourse," 52.

47 Foucault, "Truth and Power," 131.

48 According to Foucault, ideology is an insufficient concept for three reasons. The first, and for my analysis the most important, is that ideology "always stands in opposition to something which is supposed to stand for truth. ... the problem does not consist in drawing the line between that in a discourse which falls under the category of scientificity or truth, and that which comes under some other category, but in seeing historically how effects of truth are produced within discourses which in themselves are neither true nor false. The second drawback is that the concept of ideology refers ... to something of the order of a subject. Thirdly, ideology stands in a second-

line between science or truth and that which falls into another category, but[49] to illustrate how the effects of truth, the effects of the self-evident, are formed within discourse. After all, truth, as Foucault reiterates, is not "outside power"[50] and it is not "the reward of free spirits, the child of protracted solitude, nor the privilege of those who have succeeded in liberating themselves."[51] I am trying to show what truth actually is. And what is truth if not power?[52] Therefore, in my project I do not pose the question of the reality of power/truth, but the use of its effectiveness.

Let us discuss further the nature of power, which in understanding the metaburek is still somehow reasonable to understand using the framework of Foucault's conceptual coordinates. Power, as has been indicated not only by Foucault, but also by Antonio Gramsci and Edward Said,[53] is also productive. And not just legally and negatively; it does not say only what we may not do, but also technically and positively; it enables us to do things. Foucault's oft-repeated argument is that power merely constructs the thing that is to be the subject of repression. It creates knowledge, discourses, meanings, practices, rules, self-evidence. The power written into the truth and self-evidence of healthy lifestyles creates a series of dialogues, phrases and warnings about the unhealthiness and greasiness of bureks, numerous professional, scientific, and fictional texts with the burek playing the role of the (fattening, unhealthy) scapegoat, advice from professionals and various professionals regarding the eating of bureks, new burekrecipes (i.e. the

---

ary position relative to something that functions as its infrastructure, as its material, economic determinant, etc." (Foucault, "Truth and Power," 118.)

49 This is the "but" referred to in footnote 39.

50 Foucault, "Truth and Power," 131.

51 Ibid.

52 The "political economy of truth" in modern societies is characterized, following Foucault, "Truth and Power," 131, by the following attributes: truth depends on scientific discourse and the institutions that produce it; it is subject to continuous political and economic stimulation; it is defined extremely broadly and in consumerist terms (through educational and informational structures); it is produced under the supervision of large political and economic structures (universities, the military, the media); it is a subject of political debate and social confrontation (so-called ideological warfare).

53 See Edward Said, *Orientalism* (London: Penguin, 2003).

"low-fat cheese burek"), healthier ways to prepare bureks and so on. But before we continue to list them it seems that we must at least to some extent offer the metaburek, which has until now been entirely subordinate to discourse, to that on which discourse actually operates.

We have spoken of power, which up to this point could be understood as a centralized entity. But I think that at least for the purposes of the analysis of the metaburek it would be more appropriate to decentralize it. From here on we shall refer rather to relationships of power.

According to Foucault, power relations are defined by two irreplaceable elements: that the thing on which power is exercised is entirely recognized as an entity which acts, and that a number of responses, consequences, reactions, etc. can be formed against power.[54] "In effect, what defines a relationship of power is that it is a mode of action which does not act directly and immediately on others. Instead it acts upon their actions: an action upon an action."[55] Therefore it is a case of acting upon actions, both actual existing ones as well as potential ones.

Therefore we have to deal with subjects which have the possibility of forming various reactions. We can respond differently to dietary recommendations, ads for yogurt with 0.0% fat, waif-like fashion models. To stay with familiar examples, we can start baking low-fat cheese bureks or never put one in our mouth again or go out and get the greasiest burek and make jokes at the expense of sponsor-laden, annoying healthy lifestyles.

According to Foucault then, power cannot be possessed; it is simply a kind of strategy, a network of relationships. Power also cannot be localized and cannot be analyzed as the product of a conscious inclination or interest. Also, one cannot get away from power, but it is possible to set certain power strategies against others.

A little earlier we spoke of the nature of power. We said that it was productive. To this we can add that it is also mobile and indeterminate.

54 Michel Foucault, "The Subject and Power," in *Michel Foucault: Beyond Structuralism and Hermeneutics*, ed. Hubert L. Dreyfus and Paul Rabinow (New York: Harvester Wheatsheaf, 1983), 219–222.

55 Ibid, 220.

Such a nature and understanding of power also implies a singular approach to an analysis of power. It would be too much to expect an analysis of the legal superstructure of sovereignty, state apparatuses and the ideologies which accompany them. It would also be wrong to expect an analysis of the legitimate and regular forms of power in its central locations and the general effects through which they act. Where can we go with this kind of understanding of power? I think mainly towards revealing power at its edges, in those places where it becomes, to use Foucault's vocabulary, capillary. Therefore, primarily through an analysis of power beyond legal regulations, through an analysis of the investment of power in institutions, embodied in various techniques and relationships with material circumstances. "[W]e are not searching for the headquarters," since we are all "part of the character of large, nameless, nearly mute strategies."[56]

And as already stated, this understanding of power also dictates a unique understanding of the subject within power relations. Translated very freely from the semiotic language of Roland Barthes: connotation[57] is not just a tool of repression, an ideological illusion in the hands and possession of the rulers (in his opinion the bourgeoisie), as Barthes understood it. Connotation is also an emancipating tool in the hands of the subjugated. It is a tool, a strategy which is available to everyone who is caught in a relationship of power, since power, according to Foucault, "is exercised only over free subjects, and only insofar as they are free."[58]

---

56 Foucault, *The History of Sexuality*, 99.

57 Denotation means the basic, descriptive level of meaning on which the majority of members of a certain culture agree. On this level the word "burek" means a dish made of phyllo dough with various fillings. Connotation on the other hand refers to the broader level of meaning in a certain culture: values, ideologies, viewpoints and so on are attached to meaning. The word "burek" on this secondary, connotative level in the phraseme "You're a burek" means something inferior, mentally unenviable, a worthless entity, in short a loser. At the level of sign structure it can be viewed as follows: The signifier (the spoken or written word "burek") and the signified (the mental concept of a burek) form the sign (denotation), which becomes a new signifier at the next, abstract level of cultural meanings (connotation) (see Roland Barthes, *Mythologies*, trans. Richard Howard and Annette Lavers [New York: Hill and Wang, 2012]). As Barthes says elsewhere, "The connotators do not fill the whole of the lexia, reading them does not exhaust it. ... [T]here always remain[s] in the discourse a certain denotation without which, precisely, that discourse would not be possible." (Barthes, "The Rhetoric of the Image," in *Image—Music—Text* [London: Fontana Press, 1977], 50.)

58 Foucault, "The Subject and Power," 221.

Therefore in this project we will not set the metaburek into a semiotic dictatorship, but onto a battlefield, into a battle for meaning, into "semiotic warfare."[59] "Burek? Nein danke" does not live an easy, peaceful, carefree life. How could it, if it can be parodied so cruelly by saying, as it was in the title of one of the numerous Slovene articles about bureks, "Burek? Ja, bitte!"

The Metaburek and (Non-)Interpretation

Meaning, which Jonathan Culler called "the very furniture of the world," that "social fact,"[60] however represents a singular problem for discursive analysis, a problem which originates in the slippery nature of meaning. Barthes' concept of connotation enables the loosening or even the end of the structuralist idea of a single, natural and unique meaning.[61] As Jacques Derrida later demonstrated, a text is never received as it was sent.[62] Meaning constantly changes with respect to context, historical time, use, and addressee.

Words, texts, pictures, images, actions, and things always have only a certain relative meaning. We can never precisely know what meaning a certain statement has for a certain individual, since it is continuously reformed in interaction with him. For the majority of people the phraseme "You're a burek" is an insult, but for young people it can be a term of endearment.

In the language of structural linguistics, the relationship between the signifier (the spoken or written word) and the signified (the mental concept of a burek) is not written in stone (as we can see in the phrase "You're a burek"). Signifying is therefore an endless process, and meanings cannot be fixed to any point of origin. But if meaning changes in

---

59 The expression "semiotic warfare" is used by John Fiske (cited in Jim McGuigan, *Cultural Populism* [London, New York: Routledge, 1993], 73).

60 Jonathan Culler, *Saussure* (Hassocks; Sussex: The Harvester Press, 1976), 71.

61 Barthes' concept of connotation also dethroned the romantic obsession with the role of the author as the privileged interpreter of meaning. Texts of course have many more meanings than authors intend or want.

62 Jacques Derrida, *Of Grammatology*, trans. Gayatri Chakravorty Spivak (Baltimore; London: The Johns Hopkins University Press, 1976).

time and space and is never completely determined, as established by Stuart Hall, then the changing of meaning has to be included in the current process of interpretation. In every instance of interpretation there is a constant fluctuation of meaning, and thus interpretation becomes a crucial aspect of the process, as Hall continues, by which we attribute and accept meaning.[63] Interpretation therefore by definition never produces a final, absolute truth. And as Nietzsche said: there are no great truths, there are only interpretations.[64]

Interpretation in this analysis of the metaburek does not mean the discovering of hidden meaning. The difficulty of such an endeavour—searching for hidden meaning—is that the more we interpret things the more we realize that there is no concrete, absolute meaning of things, only other, different and ever new interpretations. As Foucault put it even more radically: "If interpretation is a never-ending task, it is simply because there is nothing to interpret."[65]

Our analysis will mainly concern the collection and documentation of interpretations. Discourses, as one of Foucault's interviewers put it slightly recklessly, need no interpretation, no one to assign them a meaning.[66] Such an activity—the documenting of interpretations—is therefore set in opposition to the search for and discovery of unchangeable, eternal truths. Such an activity implies, supports and establishes entirely the opposite project: the tearing down and destruction of ideal meanings and eternal truths. And here we are unavoidably faced with the analysis of power relations. When we hear talk of meanings, truths, and values, we are seeing the reflections of relationships of power, dominion, and authority.

Of course a certain minimal level of interpretation is required. Without it, it would actually be impossible to recognize meanings and the process of signification. A statement is not "something simply and

63 Stuart Hall, "The Work of Representation," in *Representation: Cultural Representations and Signifying Practices*, ed. Stuart Hall (Sage: London, 2002), 53.

64 Once again one of Nietzsche's leitmotifs is at work here, which is to a great extent covered by the one from the beginning of the chapter "Towards the Burek" and which is also well-described by Nietzsche's comments in the footnote. So instead of a new one, let's go back to footnote 2.

65 Cited in Hubert L. Dreyfus and Paul Rabinow, *Michel Foucault: Beyond Structuralism and Hermeneutics* (Chicago: The University of Chicago Press, 1982), 107.

66 Michel Foucault, "Truth and Power," 115.

directly given, which could be seen by the naked eye—to get to it you have to dig, even though it's right on the surface."[67]

At this point, when it seems as if everything is kind of hazy, and we are jumping from concept to concept, from theory to theory, and from truth to truth, let's clear something up. The intention of this introduction, oriented as it is towards the burek, is not to give a general overview of the various epistemological approaches, theories, methodologies and all of the other scientific apparatus, all the flotsam and jetsam which in one way or another concerns the issue of and the conceptualization of the metaburek. It is simply a presentation and establishment of the concepts, tools, approaches and methodologies that I myself will be using. For better or worse—of course depending on interpretation—my job is to make sure that the approach is eclectic and that the object of the analysis is not given in advance. As Edward Said said, "there is no such thing as a merely given, or simply available, starting point: beginnings have to be made for each project in such a way as to *enable* what follows from them."[68] But let's discuss this in a separate chapter.

The Burek and the Metaburek (Part II)

The burek is a reflection of the entire world.

This is undoubtedly an exaggeration. But that is just what the situation requires. The metaburek has an inclination towards exaggeration, change, manipulation, trickery, modification. In short, towards creativity. The metaburek is actually a funny thing. We might compare it to the double body of a king. Or with his ideal body, which in comparison to the ephemeral body—subject to birth and death—does not pass with time and is maintained as the infallible and untouchable embodiment of the kingdom.[69]

67 Mladen Dolar, "Spremna beseda," xiii.

68 Edward Said, *Orientalism*, 16.

69 The duality of the king's body is discussed by Ernst Kantorowicz (*The King's Two Bodies: A Study in Mediaeval Political Theology* [Princeton: Princeton University Press, 1970]), and Foucault (*Discipline and Punish*, 29) then elaborates it into an analogy with the soul. Around this duality he organizes

We could also compare the metaburek with the body of a convict: with that part of the body which has legal status, demands its ritual and triggers an entire theoretical discourse. Foucault, who used this analogy to illustrate one of the objects of his analysis, states that additional power causes the king's body to become double. He asks himself whether the absolute power exercised over the convict's body does not lead to a further doubling, a doubling with the non-corporeal, with the soul. The soul, which like the metaburek is not a substance and is not corporeal, but is real, "is the element in which are articulated the effects of a certain type of power. And the reference of a certain type of knowledge, the machinery by which the power relations give rise to a possible corpus of knowledge, and knowledge extends and reinforces the effects of this power."[70]

The metaburek, like the soul, is not an illusion or an ideological effect. But it exists, it has a certain reality, it is constantly on the surface. However, in comparison with the soul, and with the king's intransient body, there is an important difference. The metaburek is not a part of a duality with the convict's body or the king's intransient body, but with the burek. That is, the unconditioned burek.

Of course we could describe the metaburek differently, for instance, to cite Dick Hebdige, as "a crime against the natural order."[71] The metaburek is therefore a product of the process of cultivating the burek, raising the burek from the level of nature to the level of culture. In even more technical, order-seeking language, we could say that the metaburek is a "marking service," as Mary Douglas and Baron Isherwood described the difference between the utilitarian value of food and its embeddedness in culture,[72] and that the unconditioned burek is a "physical service." Of course this product and process of re-education, this "crime against the natural order," this entangled growth, this knot

---

the iconography and political theory of monarchy, the legal mechanisms that separate the king's person from the demands of the crown and at the same time bind him to them, and even the rituals, the most significant of which are the coronation, the funeral and the ceremonies of submission.

70 Foucault, *Discipline and Punish*, 29.

71 Dick Hebdige, *Subculture: The Meaning of Style* (London; New York: Methuen & Co., 1979), 3.

72 See Mary Douglas and Baron Isherwood, *The World of Goods: Towards an Anthropology of Consumption* (London; New York: Routledge, 1996).

in the web of culture, can be defined and also theoretically processed in different ways.

In this analysis we will understand the metaburek primarily as the *product* of objective possibilities, communications channels and power relations. The analysis of the metaburek will thus include three types of closely interwoven streams: possibility/communication/power. Let's take that high-school snack, the greasy burek. This activity is carried out with the help of a series of regular communications (differentiating value marks, levels of knowledge, coded signs), within a framework of numerous power relations and processes (defiance of parental and school authority, opposition to certain forms of knowledge) and of course within a framework of objective possibilities (the accessibility of the burek in terms of price, space, time, etc.).

Of course, in some cases power relations are pre-eminent (e.g. in the case of the non-appearance of the burek in Slovenia's number one cultural institution Cankarjev dom), while in others the circumstances dominate (e.g. the burek as a student snack food), and sometimes communications channels are the primary factor (e.g. in the phraseme "You're a burek").

Here I would like to state quite clearly that this project is not about analyzing power relations, communications aspects and objective possibilities. It is an analysis of an object which is subject to them. Of this "crime against the natural order," of this creative state of subjectivity, which is no ordinary crime, and no ordinary subjectivity. It is a unique and unrepeatable crime against the unconditioned burek, a unique and irreversible state of subjectivity, which establishes, forms, and generates the metaburek.

It is thus an analysis of the burek's soul, the intransient element in which the effects of specific power relations, communications channels and objective possibilities are articulated.

Undoubtedly the analysis of the metaburek involves more than just various analytical and/or methodological pre-eminences. The very nature of the metaburek dictates an analytical postulate, the pre-eminence of the discursive over the non-discursive. But this pre-eminence, at least in the analysis of the metaburek as we have framed it, cannot mean reductions, may not implicate, as Jože Vogrinc put it, a "vulgar idealism."[73] Discourse is not independent of objective possibility and history. It is both historically and objectively conditioned.

The primacy of the semantic over the pragmatic is more methodologically conditioned. The predominance of the analysis of textuality, of linguistic statements, has to be sought on one hand in the mere fact of preservation and numbers, and on the other hand in the explicitness and directness of textuality. And we will undoubtedly discover a few more primacies when we talk...

---

73 Jože Vogrinc, "Raymond Williams in navadna kultura" [Raymond Williams and Ordinary Culture], in *Navadna kultura: izbrani spisi* [Ordinary Culture: Selected Essays] by Raymond Williams (Ljubljana: Studia humanitatis, 1998), 289–290.

About the Burek

The Burek is Great and/or a Nutritious Junk Food: on the burek and healthy lifestyles

Nutritious junk food

In an article titled "Prizren Bureks from a Slovenian Street" published in *Večer* way back in 1966, we read: "A good burek is a light, healthy, caloric, and cheap food."[1] The burek—a light healthy food?[2]

In the abstract of a diploma thesis entitled *The Meat Burek in Nutrition, an Analysis of Quality and Proposal for Improvement* from 1991, author Gordana Vulić states the following:

> *Meat bureks were received from three private and three socially-owned producers, five times. These six samples and one home-made sample were tested for content of water, ash, fats, protein, sodium, potassium, iodine, sensory analysis and calculation of caloric value. On the basis of the results of the analysis and statistical processing, differences were detected in the quality of the individual samples between private and socially-owned producers*

1 B. P., "Prizrenski Burek iz Slovenske ulice" [Prizren Bureks from a Slovenian Street], *Večer*, May 18, 1966, 4.

2 Until the nineteen-nineties—at least in *Večer*, the only Slovene newspaper that has converted all of its materials into digital format, thus allowing fast searching using keywords—the burek was not considered an unwholesome, unhealthy food. In fact we can find quite a few approving burekstatements associated with health. However, there are too few of them to allow for a detailed and reliable analysis of the genesis of such assertions. The discursive rupture—if there was in fact a rupture—remains wrapped in fog.

and the nutritional value of the products. A comparison of the chemical content and the results of sensory analysis of the home-made sample with the other samples indicates the possibility of a better product with respect to the selection and reduced proportion of fats, reduced proportion of added NaCl and increased proportion of meat. This leads to a better overall impression and improved acceptability of the product. In this way the caloric value of the product is reduced, the proportion and quality of proteins is increased, the proportion of saturated fatty acids is reduced, the sodium content of the burek is reduced and the sensory qualities of the burek are improved. All of this leads to the nutritional and physiological acceptability of the burek for everyday nutrition.[3]

But in the chapter entitled "Discussion," the graduate of the Department of Food Science and Technology at the Faculty of Biotechnology of the University of Ljubljana takes more than just the chemical content and sensory qualities of the burek to task. Longer serving times and falling temperatures, she continues, can lead to decreases in sensory and nutritional quality and to the development of pathogenic microflora.[4] But that's not all:

In a hygienic and nutritional sense the next phase—eating—is also questionable. With a meat burek you can satisfy your hunger cheaply, quickly and fairly tastily, but this style of eating (in an unhygienic environment) gives one only a feeling of fullness, but not a feeling of satisfaction and a good feeling during and after the meal. For this reason the meat burek is only accepted by a part of the population in our environment. Therefore major changes have to be made in production and products in order to come closer to modern fast food and expand the consumer base. The following has to be achieved:

---

3 Gordana Vulić, "Mesni burek v prehrani, analiza kvalitete in predlog za izboljšanje" [The Meat Burek in Nutrition, an Analysis of Quality and Proposal for Improvement] (BA diss., University of Ljubljana, 1991), iii.

4 Vulić, "Mesni burek," 49.

- *consistent quality of all raw materials and taste preparation,*
- *standardized size, shape and composition,*
- *imaginative combinations of different foods which are sources of vitamins and ballast substances,*
- *vendors must give customers the opportunity to enjoy their meals in a clean, comfortable and relaxed environment with fast and friendly service,*
- *the price has to be competitive with respect to classical foods,*
- *has to satisfy the principle of HEALTHY FOOD.*

We require that healthy food among other things is correctly distributed throughout the day. For many people a meat burek takes the place of breakfast, lunch or dinner or is just a snack when very hungry before the main meal. In the majority of cases it is inappropriate; it is "too small" for a main course and "too big" for a snack.[5]

Gordana Vulić's text is meaningful from the perspective of how a certain form of knowledge, in this case dietetic scientific discourse,[6]

---

5 Vulić, "Mesni burek," 50. Emphasized words and phrases in cited texts are products of the author's burekstatements.

6 According to theoreticians like Anthony Giddens (*The Consequences of Modernity* [Cambridge: Polity Press, 1990]) or Ulrich Beck (*Risk Society: Towards a New Modernity*, trans. Mark Ritter [London: Sage, 1992]), the modern increase in concern for the body, health and nutrition can be understood as an individualized response to the increasing complexity of social events, which force the individual out of political and social decision-making. This shift, apparently controllable, is an individualized experience which is at the same time a social presentation of individual responsibility to the self and to society at large. A responsibility which is manifested (and judged) at the societal level in indicators of a(n) (un)healthy body. The emphasis on individual survival strategies has its roots in the decline of the social state at the end of the eighties, a lack of funds for social security and healthcare and the related promotion by medical professionals and the state of individual responsibility for health. Medical discourse, which is among the most dominant in modern Western societies, is conspicuously pervasive in everyday life as do popular, lifestyle, journalistic and many other discourses, which have been addressed by numerous authors (see Tanja Kamin, "Promocija zdravja kot mit opolnomočenega državljana" [The Promotion of Health as the Myth of the Empowered Citizen] [PhD diss., University of Ljubljana, 2004], 89). According to Kevin White (*An Introduction to the Sociology of Health and Wellness* [London: Sage, 2002], 48) the medicalization of everyday practices poses the question of whether the individual actually wants every aspect of his life to be medicalized—his personality, love life, marriage, children. We can ask ourselves here whether it is only questions that are posed to the individual. Are not the responses also forced on him to a great extent?
A rupture in Slovene discourse on the promotion of health occurred in the nineties when, according to Kamin, a period of intensive growth in health promotion messages began which are oriented towards the individual and which correspond to the shift towards the new, abovementioned approach to health safety. Although the author speaks mainly about the promo-

attempts to dominate and represent even utterly trivial subjects, e.g. the size of a burek.

The burek appears to be a particularly good example. It is highly visible, and is something of a sightseeing attraction, especially in comparison with other foods. It is popular[7]—in a column on national brands, *Delo* [Slovenia's leading newspaper] columnist Boris Jež wrote: "When Time magazine presented the ten national dishes of the ten new members of

---

tion of health, the nineties were also accompanied by a noticeable influx of medicinal discourse into everyday life. Slovenian public opinion research indicates that from that point on people have been increasingly concerned with health, engaged in increasing amounts of recreation, consumed increasing amounts of "healthy" food, have made increasing numbers of preventive trips to the doctor's office, fewer people are smokers etc. (see Niko Toš and Brina Malnar, "Stališča o zdravju in zdravstvu: analiza rezultatov raziskav iz obdobja 1994–2001" [Views of Health and Healthcare: An Analysis of Research Results in the Period 1994–2001], in *Družbeni vidiki zdravja* [Social Aspects of Health], ed. Niko Toš and Brina Malnar [Ljubljana, FDV; IDV; Center za raziskovanje javnega mnenja in množičnih komunikacij, 2002], 91–94). We can also see an increase in editorial and medical content dealing either implicitly or explicitly with health. *Zdravje* [Health] magazine, published since 1978 and using the last read method in the second half of 2005 reaching 169,000 readers per month, ranking it in an "excellent" third place among monthlies on the Slovenian market, was joined in December 1993 by *Viva* magazine, subtitled "Magazine for a Healthy Life," and in March 2004 by the monthly *Lepa in zdrava* [Beautiful and Healthy]. In addition, several Slovenian dailies began introducing special supplements on health, and more space was given to health matters in lifestyle magazines and in numerous other media in general. It would probably also be possible to detect a large growth in health content in other areas in the public (e.g. advertising) and private spheres (e.g. informal conversations).

The medicalization of everyday life is undoubtedly to a very great extent responsible for the growth of interest in (healthy) food. In this context I should mention that the above-mentioned magazines allocate a large amount of space to healthy food. But the increased interest in food did not materialize; it is articulated only in medical discourse. Here I should also mention the increasing importance of one's bodily appearance, the increased importance of leisure activities (which include cooking and eating), and the increased stylization of life, within which (light) food holds a very significant position.

7 Some numerical data on burekpopularity (the popularity of the burek in Slovenia in comparison with other fast food). In a telephone survey by the daily newspaper *Delo* it took second place (14.3%) behind the winner, "pizza by the slice" (27.1%) and ahead of hamburgers (11.1%), sandwiches (8.6%), French fries (7.1%), hot dogs (4.4%) and kebabs (4.2%). In urban environments there are (as could be expected) significantly more burek, hamburger and kebab fans, while in rural areas pizza and French fries enjoy above average popularity. The proportion of bureklovers also increases with the level of education of the respondents. Among people with higher education the burek even trumps pizza and takes first place at 23.3%, with pizza in second place at one per cent lower. The telephone survey asked: "Which of the following is your favourite type of fast food?"; "Which is your least favourite fast food?"; "Which fast food seems the least healthy to you?" They also asked what kind of burek was the respondents' favourite. The most popular was the cheese burek (47.3%), followed by meat (16.7%), apple (10.6%) and pizza burek (4.7%). The telephone survey was conducted on 25 February 2005 on a sample of 406 people. The article does not state whether the sample was representative, but it is clear that it was not conducted solely in an urban environment, which is the usual "home" of fast food (see Nejc Pal, "Mesni ali sirni? Sirni" [Meat or Cheese? Cheese], *Večer*, March 4, 2005, 13).

the European Union, it chose *potica* [one of the most popular desserts in Slovenia, made of leavened dough and usually filled with a nut filling] for Slovenia, which is in fact fashionable again, but we eat a thousand times less of it than we do burek."[8] It is a food of the youth, who a priori eat "unhealthily," as we can read in an article about school lunches: "It would perhaps be different with leftovers [in schools] if they were to take into account primarily the children's wishes, but then the most common things on the menu would be pizza, cheese burek, and ice cream (instead of milk and cocoa)."[9] It is inexpensive, as we are told by the title of an article about the car theft business: "In the morning not enough for a burek, in the evening 30,000 dollars in your pocket."[10] It has a lowly status in nutritional ideology—in an interview about status-related consumption habits, sociologist Gregor Tomc gives the following example: "Food for instance has a utility value. But it's not the same if you eat a burek on Miklošičeva Street in Ljubljana or shrimp at the pri Asu restaurant [an upscale eatery in downtown Ljubljana]."[11] And it has a lowly status in general—we return to the *Delo* columnist, but from a different column, in which he rails against the "decline" of the coast:

> *Portorož [the number one tourist destination on the Slovene coast] at least used to have the Slovene elite—God knows it wasn't very rich, but it figured as an elite and it made Portorož what it was. A concept. Once you could even buy paintings here, not just čevapčiči and bureks. The place has sold out in the broad sense, including the exuberant creativity of its people. Now everything has been reduced to a few ice cream sellers, cheap jewellery hawkers and boutiques; the place has lost its shine.*[12]

---

8 Boris Jež, "Bo Martin Strel naša blagovna znamka?" [Will Martin Strel Be Our National Trademark?], *Delo, Sobotna priloga*, July 3, 2004, 23.

9 Mimi Podkrižnik, "Kakšno hrano jedo otroci v šoli?" [What Kind of Food Do Our Children Eat in School?], *Delo*, April 18, 2000, 10.

10 Bruno Kuzmin, "Zjutraj nimaš za burek, zvečer je v žepu 30.000 dolarjev" [In the Morning Not Enough for a Burek, in the Evening 30,000 Dollars in Your Pocket], *Delo*, June 7, 2003, 17.

11 Grega Repovž, "Tekma poceni denarja" [A Race for Easy Money], *Delo, Sobotna priloga*, March 31, 2001, 8.

12 Boris Jež, "Galerija, črpalka, trgovina ... Smo se za to borili?" [A Gallery, a Gas Station, a Shop... Is This What We Were Fighting For?], *Delo, Sobotna priloga*, June 19, 2004, 13.

To put up a little resistance against this media dictatorship, let's juxtapose that last example with a statement from the Slovenian National Assembly: "Elan [a Slovenian sporting goods manufacturer, (once) the pride of Slovenian industry and a brand with which Slovenes quickly identify], which is no small thing, like, I don't know, selling bureks in a kiosk in Zgornja Kungota, but Elan [...]."[13] But let's return to Gordana Vulić's text. It is also meaningful in the way it plays roles and represents a series of different characters: "changes have to be made," "we require that healthy food," "the following has to be achieved". It speaks on behalf of a certain absolute knowledge, but in no way does it speak on behalf of those who actually eat bureks, who (perhaps) don't care at all about calories, fat or "healthy food" or who simply don't have the time, energy, money, or patience for something "better" or "healthier." Burek eaters simply don't know what's good for them. As Karl Marx said, "They cannot represent themselves, they must be represented."[14]

Having knowledge about such matters means that you master them, that you have authority over them. Authority from such a self-satisfied, imperious position—a position that uses "scientific", scientistic arguments[15]—means the denial of "their" autonomy, i.e. the people who eat unhealthy food, burek eaters. So it is no surprise that the text overlooks or fails to ask whether burek eaters even have the possibility of eating a "nutritionally correct" meal. To nutritional science it probably seems superfluous, debasing and dishonourable to ask who eats bureks, in what circumstances and why.

The burek has thus become a subject of discourse with scientific status. In scientific and professional nutritional discourse (nutritional and

---

13 Janez Drobnič, accessed August 27, 2007, http://www.dz-rs.si/index.php?id=97&cs=1&mandate=3&unid.=SZA3%7C0BB452F81225B7ACC1256EBB0030795F&showdoc=1.

14 Karl Marx, *The Eighteenth Brumaire*, 106.

15 Science and/or scientism? Science in the true sense of the word produces unconditional products, or as Jože Vogrinc states in his written commentary to my doctoral thesis (the entire differentiation between science and scientism which follows is taken from Vogrinc): those which are produced "[f]rom a love of knowledge, truth, production without a reason." And these products of science are attainable through various discourses and praxes. Scientism on the other hand is an ideology which attributes a higher knowledge to science. So, or better, therefore, it uses scientific arguments as rhetorical devices. "Science"—in quotation marks and in the first person singular—appears in the position of authority, which it can only do if in fact it is used by authority. "Science" is therefore academic disciplines in the service of the wielders of power.

medical science, articles with medical and nutritional findings, reports, instructions) the burek ranks low on the list of healthy foods. The burek is therefore not healthy food; it stands opposite to it, but not always so clearly, openly and profoundly as described above. In an article about the energy density of fast food published in the scientific journal *Zdravstveno varstvo* [Health Care]—the Slovenian magazine that publishes the highest number of medical and nutritional scientific and professional articles about food and nutrition—the burek like all other fast food was measured as having substantially excessive energy density. In this article, fast food and with it also indirectly the burek was—without reference to other research or sources—charged with having other harmful properties (excessive total energy, whole and saturated fats as well as cholesterol, salt and sugar).[16] Dr. Dražigost Pokorn, Slovenia's foremost authority on food from the healthcare perspective, characterized the burek (as well as other fast food) as "empty."[17] In an article on the nutritional habits of Ljubljana eighth-graders in *Zdravstveno varstvo*, the burek finds itself in the company of other fast foods (hamburgers, French fries, hot dogs, *pleskavica*), which is a priori, without reference to scientific findings or research, characterized as "monotonous."[18]

This "scientific" authority on fast food, and on the burek, seems, to use the words of Edward Said, "instrumental [and] persuasive; [...] it is virtually indistinguishable from certain ideas it dignifies as true, and from traditions, perceptions and judgments it forms, transmits, reproduces."[19]

This "scientific" healthy-lifestyle discourse however does not meditate in a hermetically sealed ivory tower. In other words, its great thoughts do not shine only on the apparently inwardly-focused world of scientific texts. Medical and dietetic discourse radiate out into many fields. And this radiation is no innocent thing, without consequences, without impacts on other things. The following excerpt from a

16 Ana Hojs, "Energijska gostota hitre hrane" [The Energy Density of Fast Food], *Zdravstveno varstvo* 37 (1998): 47–50.

17 Dražigost Pokorn, telephone conversation, 30 May, 2006.

18 Meta Medved et al., "Prehrambne navade ljubljanskih osmošolcev" [Eating Habits among Primary School Children in Ljubljana], *Zdravstveno varstvo* 37 (1998): 312.

19 Said, *Orientalism*, 19.

journalist's article gives us an insight into the mechanisms of the regulation of school nutrition:

> *At last night's round table at the Office of Education, the Children and Youth Nutrition Working Group (Dr. Dražigost Pokorn, Dr. Irena Simčič (Chair), Dr. Verena Koch and Dr. Maruša Adamič), which is part of the National Program Council for Healthy Lives of Schoolchildren, discussed guidelines for healthy nutrition in schools. They agree that the meals are not to everyone's taste, but the schools are also conducting surveys in which the children say what they would like to eat. It is not surprising, says Verena Koch, that the children would most prefer to eat hamburgers, baked potatoes, chips, etc. But these are wishes that do not belong on a balanced elementary school menu. A proper menu would include [...].*[20]

Dr. Verena Koch, who among other things teaches future biology and home economics teachers at the Department of Biology, Chemistry and Home Economics of the Faculty of Pedagogy of the University of Ljubljana, as a professor of Nutrition and Special Didactics of Home Economics Education, probably listed bureks after chips (the journalist abbreviated the quotation with an ellipsis). And even if she didn't, she probably would if she had been asked. But such speculation does not belong in this "serious" scientific discussion. Therefore, let's have a look at how this debate is reflected in practice, how it affects the regulation of this nutritional degenerate:

> *According to the experience of Biserka Marolt, who works as a cashier in the kitchen of a construction, geodetics and economics secondary school, healthily prepared food does not smell good to the students. "They buy mini pizzas and bureks, they don't like vegetables, so they take them out of their sandwiches themselves, and if they don't, they throw them down the hallways," says Marolt.*

20 Aleš Čakš, "Prva želja—hamburger" [First Choice—Hamburger], *Delo*, March 21, 2001, 3.

> *They also offer them full lunches, which only the teachers take. It's different at a secondary school for teachers and gymnasium. "We cook a variety of food with a lot of fruit and dairy products; burek is on the menu at most once a month. You can't just raise the awareness of youths, sometimes you have to listen to them too," remarked Principal Milka Arko.*[21]

How attentive!

It is thus no easy task to separate the purportedly neutral and enlightened world of "science" and knowledge from power and authority. That is, knowledge is power, but it requires authority. More power and authority requires more knowledge and so on, in an increasingly profitable dialectic of information and control, knowledge and power, as Said stated.[22]

It seems that the burek has mainly negative connotations, connected to health (or rather the lack thereof), even in more popular, non-professional debates and convictions.[23] Primož Mihelič, a childhood friend who is now a highly educated thirty-year-old, blamed his gallstone operation on excessive consumption of bureks during secondary school and college and gave up eating them after the operation.[24] Primož Smerkolj, a great fan of bureks since the mid-nineteen seventies, responded as follows to the question of whether in his years of making bureks since the beginning of the nineties he had "reduced the amount or type of fat":

> *What can I tell you, I went down to 0% fat, 0% cottage cheese, 0% yogurt, 0% dough. In short, I haven't made a burek for about*

21 Maja Čakarić, "Na šolsko kosilo pridejo le učiltelji" [Only Teachers Eat the School Lunch], *Delo*, January 13, 2006, 6.

22 Said, *Orientalism*, 40.

23 In Deborah Lupton's research for her book *Food, the Body and the Self* (London: Sage, 1996) nearly all of her interviewees ranked greasy food, "junk and fast food," salty food, fatty red meat, chocolate, soft drinks, and other sweetened foods as unhealthy. Healthy food included first and foremost fruit and vegetables (particularly fresh), salad, whole grains, pasta, chicken and fish. A series of studies carried out in (post)industrial countries indicated very similar nutritional preferences—i.e. a more or less orthodox appropriation and valuation of dietetic recommendations regarding the health aspects of food (for an overview of the studies see Lupton, *Food, the Body, and the Self*, 80–82).

24 Primož Mihelič, conversation, July, 2005.

> *a year. The reason is simple: I have high blood pressure and cholesterol issues and I am trying to be a little careful, so if I don't make bureks and don't buy them, I don't eat them either.*[25]

This negative attitude towards the burek—as an unhealthy food—is also common in various media statements. In an article entitled "You need to have papers for a burek" on the removal of a burek kiosk on Krekov Square in Ljubljana, we read: "In general, shops selling burek, pleskavica and similar junk food are looking at hard times."[26] But a survey by *Delo* indicated that bureks are not that low on the junk food scale. In a telephone survey on fast food, to the question "What fast food do you consider to be the least healthy?" 406 (35.5%) of respondents put hamburgers in first place, 24.9% chose French fries, 6.2% bureks, 6.2% hot dogs, 4.9% pizza by the slice, 3% kebabs and 2.7% sandwiches.[27] It is undoubtedly significant that the respondents to this survey were given the above list of unhealthy foods. And furthermore, why wasn't the question posed positively; why didn't they ask which fast food they considered the healthiest? But the results of this survey are significant mainly due to the fact that they indicate a major gap between the survey winner, the hamburger, and the winner for most appearances in statements which focus on the unhealthy, the burek. In other words, according to the results of the survey one might expect the hamburger to have the honour of being the main signifier of unhealthy food. But this appears to be a purely subjective impression; according to my review of the electronic newspaper archives, this honour falls squarely on the shoulders of the burek.

Foreigners have also commented on the detrimental effects of the burek. Did we unwittingly teach them about the unhealthiness of the burek? In a sort of invitation to visit Slovenia in the guide *Via Stansted Express*, which is put out on the train seats for Ryanair passengers travelling from Stansted Airport to London, in addition to various

25 Primož Smerkolj, e-mail message to author, March 7, 2007.

26 Primož Knez, "Do bureka le s papirji" [You Need to Have Papers for a Burek], *Dnevnik*, November 16, 1999, 17.

27 Nejc Pal, "Mesni ali sirni? Sirni" [Meat or Cheese? Cheese], *Večer*, March 4, 2005, 13.

exhortations to visit pleasant Ljubljana coffee houses, the town market, bars and clubs, "Britons are invited to have a midday snack of burek, a local specialty made with cheese, which they can buy on the street. But it's not for people with weak hearts."[28]

In addition to health problems and issues associated with eating bureks, we should also mention the fear of obesity or (increased) concern for one's external appearance. The body is increasingly becoming an explicit physical symbol over which its owner exercises control. A fat body indicates gluttony, a lack of self-discipline, hedonism, and lack of moderation, while a thin body is a reflection of a high level of self-control and the ability to overcome bodily desires.[29] The media, advertising and fashion seem to be particularly important in setting the rules for this new bodily grammar. We are therefore speaking about an increasingly intimidating, clear, direct and all-encompassing language in which victory over the self—losing weight—is offered to the subject as an indicator that s/he is capable of success.[30] In a column entitled "Verifying Rumours" in the magazine *Nova*, an article entitled "Katarina Čas [a well-known TV presenter and actress]. Lover of Bureks and Tripe" begins:

---

28 Zora Kužet, "'Moški vikend' v Ljubljani" ['Men's Weekend' in Ljubljana], *Večer*, October 5, 2005, 35.

29 Lupton, *Food, the Body, and the Self*, 16.

30 The ideal of a thin body was created in the nineteen-seventies, when medical science and healthcare institutions began taking an anti-fat stance (see Lauren Williams and John Germov, "The Thin Ideal: Women, Food, and Dieting," in *A Sociology of Food and Nutrition: The Social Appetite*, ed. Lauren Williams and John Germov [South Melbourne: Oxford University Press, 1999], 209). I should mention that traditional societies valued a moderate to high body fat content, i.e. a fatter body. For traditional cultures the storage of body fat represented health and wealth, particularly among women. During times of crisis and disease they provided better protection and signified access to material and social resources. According to numerous anthropological studies, fatter bodies were (therefore?) also more attractive (see Jeffrey Sobal, "Sociological Analysis of the Stigmatisation of Obesity", in *A Sociology of Food and Nutrition: The Social Appetite*, ed. Lauren Williams and John Germov [South Melbourne: Oxford University Press, 1999], 187). As an interesting aside, during the October Revolution, posters and caricatures representing the bourgeois always portrayed them as fat. The modern ideal of a thin body was the subject of numerous structuralist (see Williams and Germov, "The Thin Ideal," 215–216) and poststructuralist, Foucaultian studies of the control and discipline primarily of the female body (see Chris Weedon, *Feminist Practice and Poststructuralist Theory* [Oxford; New York: Basil Blackwell, 1987]; Sandra Lee Bartky, *Femininity and Domination: Studies in the Phenomenology of Oppression* [London; New York: Routledge, 1990]; Sandra Lee Bartky, "Foucault, Femininity and the Modernization of Patriarchal Power," in *Feminism and Foucault: Reflections on Resistance*, ed. Irene Diamond and Lee Quinby [Boston: Northeastern University Press, 1988]; Williams and Germov, "The Thin Ideal").

This beauty doesn't just eat salads and low-calorie fat-free meals, but occasionally allows herself a greasy burek. "I definitely have a burek at least twice a month", said the television host, who eats them when she does not have a lot of time for lunch. "The next day I eat more vegetables, but there it is."[31]

In her first book, the character Hiacinta Novak, a kind of Slovene Bridget Jones, is constantly "fighting off the pounds," as dieting discourse likes to describe the practice. In her diary at the beginning of every day she lists her new body weight, calorie intake, etc. Monday, 9 September, a day after having a "greasy" burek and a beer, begins as follows: "152 lbs. (I can't believe it! A burek shouldn't weigh two pounds?), cigarettes: 2000 or so, calories: despite my strict resolution a lot. Scales: 0, 'cause I just threw mine in the trash."[32]

Exchanges among the scientific or professional and popular or imagined meanings of the burek seem to be numerous, even unavoidable, but they are not provable in advance. In fact I believe that it is not a case of democratic exchange, but relatively one-way traffic from "science" to the imagined or fictive. However, I believe it is necessary to cast aside all thoughts of the possibility that the great facts and truths expounded by medical and nutritional "science" can be mechanically transferred into the complex field of culture. "Scientific" interest turned the burek into unhealthy food, while culture later turned the burek into something complex and heterogeneous.

But the situation is not at all as simple as it seems. While "science" was stretching its sinister fingers towards the burek did it already occupy a visible and complex place in the field of culture? Science did not choose the burek by accident, or in some sort of lottery.

So to expand and broaden our perspective: healthy lifestyle discourse had several victims at its disposal, and in my opinion the burek in fact got the worst of it. But this selection should not be understood as

31 Anon., "Katarina Čas. Ljubiteljica bureka in vampov" [Katarina Čas. Lover of Bureks and Tripe], *Nova*, March 19, 2007, 49.

32 Aksinja Kermauner, *Dnevnik Hiacinte Novak. V znamenju Tehnice* [The Diary of Hiacinta Novak. Under the Sign of the Scales] (Miš: Dob pri Domžalah, 2003), 33.

an unfortunate accident, a coincidental occurrence in a lottery in which bureks, French fries, Carniolan sausage, chips, Vienna steaks, hamburgers and their "unhealthy" colleagues had equal bets. As stated above, the burek was and is a sightseeing attraction, it is inexpensive, it is of the street, it is eaten by a priori nutritionally unenlightened youths, and it is prepared by the suspect hands of immigrants. And in my opinion that's still not all there is to this story about healthy-lifestyle discourse. In the first half of the nineties, when this discourse probably selected it as a victim,[33] the burek had already garnered a significant place in popular culture, as we shall see from the following story. At that time other discourses had already begun to parasitize the burek. So it was no stranger to discourses; it was no newbie, tyro or greenhorn in the world of discourses. So what could be easier for healthy-lifestyle discourse than to use an already-existing, smoothly operating discursive infrastructure? Wouldn't it be easier to simply pull on this object spinning in the discursive field and thus have it spinning at full speed from the moment it arrived—without any separate infusion of energy needed to propel it—than to conceptualize and start up the entire complex anew, which would undoubtedly also include some unsuccessful attempts and the possibility that it would never actually begin to work?

It seems impossible to separate the allegedly neutral and enlightened world of science (knowledge) from culture and to understand it separately from culture. Healthy-lifestyle discourse thus has to be understood as knowledge about a (healthy) lifestyle, the body, movement, eating (and thus also about the burek), which places all of this and more into manuals, books and magazines, classrooms, television shows and ads, online chat rooms, scientific and vernacular language, research and jokes, questionnaires and literature, everyday practices, desires, values, tastes, recipes and of course in materiality, the material of the burek itself. Consciously or not, with a quietly or loudly proclaimed desire for it

---

33 It's hard to say exactly when healthy-lifestyle discourse began to reach for the burek. Without getting into greater detail about the methodological difficulties and pitfalls of looking for an answer to this question, I should merely mention that in the first half of the nineteen-nineties is marked not only by the noticeable entry of medical discourse into everyday life and popular culture (see the ridiculously long footnote at the beginning of this chapter), but also some albeit more implicit burekstatements.

to be able to be judged, disciplined, governed. And it is therefore also impossible to separate the purportedly neutral and enlightened world of science and knowledge and apparently frivolous and indifferent culture from politics, power and authority.

Healthy-lifestyle discourse thus attempts to address the burek and construct it in both the scientific, professional, institutional and the imagined, fictive, notional senses. However, I am in no way trying to say that healthy-lifestyle discourse strictly defines what can be said about the burek, but that what is often at work here is a specific network of interests, connections and associations whenever we speak, write or think about the burek.

So what are these interests, connections and associations?

While high fat content is only one of the negative characteristics or traits of the burek usually encountered in scientific and professional nutritional discourse, it seems that in lay and popular discourse it is the leading one. In current scientific and professional and popular discourse, fats, especially animal fats, until quite recently a highly valued component of food, almost without exception have the status of an "evil substance."[34] But in many examples the fear of obesity and worries about one's external appearance are probably a bigger issue than medical concerns and difficulties associated with eating fatty foods. In fact this is a tightly interwoven and often inseparable aspect, since today a thin body is understood not only as beautiful, but also as healthy.

Numerous interviewees, interlocutors and friends who told me that they do not eat bureks, or eat them only occasionally, most often stated their greasiness as the reason. Often without even having been prompted about greasiness. Marko Mrak in an email about his burek eating habits:

---

34 See Lupton, *Food, the Body and the Self*; and Williams and Germov, "The Thin Ideal". As studies conducted in western (post)industrial societies have shown, people routinely characterize fatty foods as unhealthy, particularly if the fats are visible (for an overview of studies see Lupton, *Food, the Body and the Self*, 80–82). In the seventies the medical profession, state healthcare and other authorities took an anti-fat position. Numerous other ingredients and foods have suffered a similar fate (sugar, white bread and white-collared food in general, which was valued very highly as late as the sixties).

> *I eat bureks occasionally, when my girlfriend doesn't feel like cooking. But I have to admit that burek variations have appeared such as the pizza burek... which somehow does not fit into my definition of a burek. But they are better than they used to be,* less greasy,[35] *with more filling... but basically the same, the taste, the fast service.*[36]

Ali Žerdin in an email responding to the question "Do you have any further info about 'bureks' and 'subcultures,' about bureks and 'Slovenian culture' or about bureks in general?" answered: "Yes. Bureks are too *greasy* for me."[37]

An "average person, but at the same time a major burekologist," as Franc Murešič-Lanko describes himself, when rating bureks in Slovenia, continuously refers to, assesses and evaluates their greasiness. In describing his blog project on the *Delo* website, in the "Burek blog," where one can find these ratings, he states the following: "The idea is simple. The quality of bureks varies greatly from burek stand to burek stand. The price not so much. Every time I eat a burek I will describe how it was. How *greasy*, how tasty, the shape, the price[.]" The fat content thus appears before the taste. For example, when rating a burek from the Soča snack bar in Nova Gorica he states: "Since it wasn't too *greasy*, I can say that it was among the *healthier*, and I could also call it that because it wasn't overcooked (which occurs pretty frequently)."[38]

Greasiness is also a frequent guest in numerous media burekstatements. In an article entitled "The Clothes Make the Soldier," which discusses the new Slovenian Army uniforms, we read: "The materials are a story unto themselves: the jacket, pants and skirt are made of a Teflon-coated wool/polyester blend, which is waterproof and oil-resistant. This means that it is highly stain-resistant, which is particularly welcome when snacking on a *greasy* burek or sampling the meat sauces at

35 All italics and emphasis in burekstatements are mine unless otherwise noted.

36 Marko Mrak, e-mail message to author, June 16, 2005.

37 Ali Žerdin, e-mail message to author, March 31, 2005.

38 Franc Maručč, accessed autumn 2006. http://www.delo.si/blog/ivanmars/index.php?BLOG_PATH=220&BLOG_ARCHIVE.

protocol events."[39] In an article with the playful/scary title "Tiger Tamers on the School Benches" we read the following advice to young people: "In order to acquire all these traits it is very important to exercise and eat right (you have to eat healthy food, and avoid things like fried steaks, French fries, bureks and other *greasy* and sweet junk food)."[40] In the diary of a Serbian immigrant to Slovenia, a large part of which concerns Slovenes and their attitudes towards their former countrymen, the burek does not appear in the expected semantic context:

> *Here [in Slovenia], the Balkans and everything simple in the Balkan way are somehow magically exotic, which they still classify as "thematic materials," exotics which operate subculturally and which are not accepted as their own, but alongside which they relax. With a certain nostalgia, not for the former ex-Yugoslavia, but for some archetypical, perhaps Slavic roots, in which limitless possibility resides. Sometimes it is this nostalgia that appears, sometimes nostalgia for the Habsburgs—interchangeably. Occasionally. In the same way that we don't eat bureks every day, because you have to watch your* cholesterol.[41]

In a commentary about the former manager of the Maribor Football Club Brane Oblak in the sports pages of the newspaper *Večer* we read the following:

> *At http://talk.to/braneoblak you can read a lot that is vulgar (If we catch him here, we'll castrate him),* greasy *(Oblak is a burek), doubting (Would Maribor play with a more attacking style if Oblak was on the bench?), heartrending (You showed your true sportsmanship to the people who used to love you), or conciliatory (Oblak, have mercy on us).*[42]

---

39 Domen Mal, "Obleka naredi vojaka" [The Clothes Make the Soldier], *Več*, February 6, 2004, 24.

40 Diana Zajec, "Krotilci tigrov v šolskih klopeh" [Tiger Tamers on the School Benches], *Delo*, September 4, 2000, 3.

41 Ana Ristović Čar, "Slovenščina za začetnike (situacijski slovar)" [Slovene for Beginners (A Situational Dictionary)], *Delo, Sobotna priloga*, September 20, 2003, 14.

42 Aljoša Stojič, "Oblak je faca" [Oblak is Cool], *Večer*, September 23, 1999, 19.

On the back cover of the first anthology of comic strips by artists from Eastern and Central Europe, called *Stripburek: Comics from Behind the Rusty Iron Curtain*, a special, thematic issue of the Slovenian comic magazine *Stripburger*, we find an equation for the burek with grease squared:

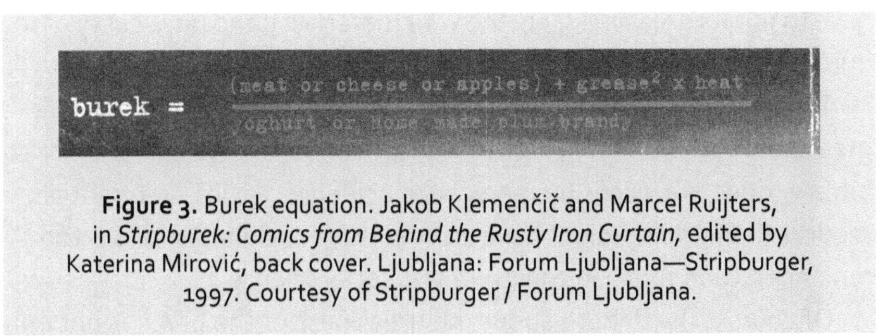

Figure 3. Burek equation. Jakob Klemenčič and Marcel Ruijters, in *Stripburek: Comics from Behind the Rusty Iron Curtain*, edited by Katerina Mirović, back cover. Ljubljana: Forum Ljubljana—Stripburger, 1997. Courtesy of Stripburger / Forum Ljubljana.

And it seems that foreigners have learned all about the greasiness of the burek. In a *Lonely Planet* guide under the title *Best of Ljubljana*, in a chapter on food where we read that there is no way bureks can be eaten elegantly, the burek receives a special box with the title "The *greasy* lowdown."[43]

We could find innumerable similar greasy declarations. Greasiness is one of the burek's most dominant and frequent connotations, probably most dominant in the company of those who underscore the material and physiological aspects of the burek.

But that's not all. The burek has become, as we saw above, an often invoked if not the most frequently invoked signifier whenever greasiness is written about, spoken of, or thought about in Slovenia. It is therefore in some way the main signifier or the signifier sine qua non of greasiness.

The greasiness of the burek is also undoubtedly the point around which—like a cat around hot porridge—healthy-lifestyle discourse circles the most, especially the part which deals with the burek in the fictive, imagined and notional sense. In other words, healthy-lifestyle

---

43 Fionn Davenport, *Best of Ljubljana: The Ultimate Pocket Guide & Map* (Footscray; Oakland; London: Lonely Planet Publications, 2006), 35.

discourse found an Achilles' heel in the burek's greasiness and directed the majority of its spears towards it. Fat—the evil substance of the new, healthy-lifestyle loving era—was discovered in the burek and a pogrom, an inquisition, a witch-hunt was undertaken with all of the requisite spectacle. When looking for an answer to the question of why Slovenian healthy-lifestyle discourse selected the burek as its victim, we have to put its greasiness, i.e. the very materiality and physicality of the burek, in the front row.

The wealth of production of meanings arising from the burek's greasiness therefore indicates that the invention of meanings is not arbitrary, does not occur by magical coincidence, is not areferential, as readers to this point might have erroneously concluded and as is too often understood today in constructivist social science.

Of course, the debate about the greasiness of the burek is not only approached directly, through statements, representations and praxis which in one way or another associate the burek with fat. The entirety of Slovenian fat discourse (recommendations and instructions for eating non-fatty foods, advertising of low-fat products, avoidance of fats, etc.) also indirectly concerns the greasiness of the burek. Even when the burek does not participate directly in these "greasy" statements, they indirectly touch upon it owing to the burek's close association with greasiness.

The focus up to this point on media statements might lead the reader to believe that healthy-lifestyle discourse reaches only into the domain of words. But this would also be an erroneous conclusion. As demonstrated by the example of the monitoring of school lunches, it is not manifested and formed solely in media statements of one form or another. If we remain on the topic of the war on fats, the anti-fat discourse, we discover very quickly how greedily it was devoured in production as well. Every bakery I talked to at least attempted to reduce fat levels. And the majority succeeded. Slovenia's two largest producers of bureks—and only manufacturers of "industrial" bureks, with automated production lines for phyllo dough and bureks—Pekarna Pečjak [the Pečjak bakery] and Žito, have used various approaches to reduce fats.[44] Pekarna Pečjak reduced the fat content of the filling. They used to use 35% fat cottage cheese in their cheese bureks, but today they use curds with 10% fat content and less fatty cream. There has also been a change in the type of fats used. When they were still producing bureks by hand, i.e. before the installation of the automated production line in 1998, they used a combination of pork fat and vegetable oil, while today they use fats of vegetable origin exclusively.[45] At Žito, Slovenia's first producer of machine-made bureks (between 1988 and 1990), they reduced the fat content of the coating by 30%, while there have been no major changes to the filling.[46] At the Orehek bakery, headquartered in Kranj, in their five years of producing bureks several attempts have been made to reduce the fat content.[47] At the Mladost ("Youth") snack bar in Velenje, where they have been making bureks since 1987, they replaced oil with vegetable shortening ten years ago. This, according to an employee, makes the burek less greasy and probably also reduces its fat content.[48] According to the owner of the Dino Burek chain, they at first used vegetable shortening, but they now use flax oil. This was also supposed to have slightly reduced the fact content.[49] And the list goes on.

They also told me that several non-commercial burek producers, both immigrants and non-immigrants, had reduced the fat content and switched to a different kind of fat. Amra Šabotić, who comes from the Bihač area in Bosnia, follows the traditional recipe for bureks or pies fairly faithfully.[50] She makes bureks for her family twice a week, and taught her fifteen-year-old elder daughter how to make them. Interestingly, in the ten years she has lived in Slovenia she has never bought a burek. But, she says, her bureks are less greasy than those

44 Slovenia's largest burekproducers Pekarna Pečjak and Žito are, according to the available data, the only commercial producers of frozen bureks in Slovenia. Both distribute frozen bureks to stores and some of the largest shopping centres, gas stations and smaller subsidiary operations which have their own ovens and thus (also) sell pre-cooked bureks or then distribute the pre-cooked bureks to schools, day-care centres, institutions, bakeries, shops etc.

45 Technician at Pekarna Pečjak, telephone conversation, 19 June, 2006.

46 Technician at Žito, telephone conversation, 5 July, 2006.

47 Director of Pekarna Orehek, telephone conversation, June, 2006.

48 Employee at the Mladost snack bar, telephone conversation, June, 2006.

49 Owner of Dino Burek, telephone conversation, 7 June, 2006.

50 For info about bureks and/or pies see the beginning of the section entitled "The Burek is Great."

in Bosnia and she uses mainly (healthier) oil instead of butter, which is the custom in Bosnia. And she has reduced the amount of fats she uses in baking in general over the past few years, so she uses less butter than she used to.[51] Gajo Vranješ, who moved to Slovenia from nearby Karlovac, Croatia, learned how to make bureks at a bakery, where he worked as a baker for several years. He usually makes bureks for dinner and has this to say about them: "Homemade bureks are the best, because you don't put so much *grease* in them."[52] Of course, this discourse is not just about "less greasy" bureks, but also deals with the quantity of bureks produced and consumed. For example, Milojka Kunarac, who moved to Slovenia from the Sandžak region in Montenegro in 1973, says: "Sometimes we put more in those pies, but now we have to be more careful."[53] She has replaced her former weekly burek with a burek every two weeks.

Before we put the final full stop to this production overview, we should mention the recipe for a "sirow low fat burek" (the use of a "w" is a humorous version of the usual Slovene "sirov," i.e. "[made of] cheese," parallelling the "ow" in "low") made of whole wheat phyllo dough (which, according to the recipe, is available at Hofer stores—an Austrian chain) with unstrained light curds, light cottage cheese ("Cottage Cheese 0.9% milk fats"), two eggs and no other (listed) fats. This recipe is available on the website "Maxximum portal," which is "intended to provide information about sports and healthy nutrition, fitness, and bodybuilding" and emblazoned with the slogan "Dedicated to a Fit Philosophy." A slice of burek with 329.5 calories contains 32.5 g of protein, 34.1 g carbohydrates and 6.4 g of fat.[54] Pedantic and healthy!

However, as several producers maintain, the quality or essence of a burek is closely or even completely inseparably associated with fats. A technician at Žito says: "We tried to reduce the fat content, but it just wasn't a burek anymore."[55] Not exactly a fortuitous discovery for the burek, eh?

---

51 Amra Šabotić, conversation, summer, 2006 and spring, 2007.
52 Gajo Vranješ, telephone conversation, summer, 2006.
53 Milojka Kunarac, conversation, summer, 2006.
54 Staša Grom, accessed July 12, 2006, http://www.maxximum-portal.com/313.html.
55 Technician at Žito, telephone conversation, July 5, 2006.

But as interviewees occasionally point out and as their statements testify, bureks are not equally greasy. And this differentiation, as we will see, is the basis for new meanings. Bureks from bakeries and industrial plants are considered less greasy than bureks from Albanian street vendors. Several people told me that they buy bureks from bakeries and industrial plants more often because they are less greasy. The actor Jernej Kuntner, in a supplement to *Viva* magazine entitled "My Refrigerator—A Window on the World," while disclosing the secrets of his diet admitted that he "also [likes] meat bureks, which he has recently been buying from bakeries rather than from kiosks, because he realized that they are noticeably less *greasy*."[56] Self-styled burekologist Franc Marušič says that bureks from the Damajanty Seam bakery in Ljubljana: "are, (or at least the ones I tried were) too typically bakery-like, that is, *non-greasy* and cooked too dry and hard."[57]

A completely different dimension, also or primarily on the level of meaning, is present when distinguishing between bureks which are not subject to examination, i.e. bureks made at home, and fast-food bureks. This differentiation insinuates itself into the introduction to the "Overview of Statements" in the above-mentioned nutritionism-faith-based diploma thesis by Gordana Vulić:

> *Meat bureks or bureks with meat have also entered into our everyday diets unnoticed. They have found their place among hot dogs, sausages, sandwiches and other similar foods. [...] However, each of us has reached for these products at least once; depending on our luck in selecting the right producer, the product is accepted or rejected. The meat burek is a felicitous combination of meat and dough, but in the context of healthy nutrition it has several negative qualities. There is no cookbook of Yugoslav recipes which does not have a recipe for meat burek. This dish is a Balkan specialty, but we rarely find it made this way. In "Jugoslovanka kuhinja"*

56 Tili Kojič, "Mojstru za njoke dišijo tartufi" [Smell of Truffles Delights Gnocchi Master], *Viva*, January, 2003, 92.

57 Franc Marušič, accessed autumn, 2006, http://www.delo.si/blog/ivanmars/index.php?BLOG_PATH=220&BLOG_ARCHIVE.

> *[Yugoslavian Cuisine] by Novak Marković (1983), there is a recipe for making meat bureks, which is followed by example number 7, a "homemade" burek.*[58]

The author discusses this "example" as a "proposal for improvement or for the adaptation of this dish to modern principles of healthy, light and low-calorie nutrition."[59]

The Burek is Great

It seems as if it's impossible to escape from this medical, dietary, healthy-lifestyle discourse. Everyone is subject to it, both eaters and non-eaters, lovers and non-lovers of the burek, immigrants and non-immigrants… But nevertheless, at least at the level of meanings there are numerous burekstatements which oppose this dominant discourse.

It would be most appropriate, and given the contents of the preceding subchapter most fitting, to begin with immigrants and the place of the burek among them. Here we first of all have to focus on immigrants of the Muslim faith from Bosnia and Herzegovina and probably somewhat fewer Muslim immigrants from other areas of the former Yugoslavia. Although the burek is an important dish and can even be an element of gift-giving and in particular an expression of hospitality in other ethnic and national communities, it is clear that it does not play such a vital role in the manifestation and shaping of the integration of society as it does among Muslim immigrants from Bosnia and Herzegovina, and somewhat less among other Muslim immigrants.[60] The differences also

58 Gordana Vulić, *Mesni burek,* 2.

59 Gordana Vulić, *Mesni burek,* 2.

60 The importance of the burek and other pies in Bosnia and Herzegovina is in many ways comparable to the importance of rice in Japan. Both are the main components of the ethnic, national diet, and both play an important or even central role in national and ethnic (self-)recognition. Emiko Ohnuki-Tierney (*Rice as Self: Japanese Identities Through Time* [Princeton: Princeton University Press, 1993] 41–42), says that in projects of differentiating Japanese from other nations and cultures, rice is mobilized as the main weapon in the fight against the "western" obsession with meat. A similar symbolic or symbolic/strategic scope can be detected in the case of the burek and other pies in Bosnia and Herzegovina, although it has to be said that the symbolic potential of rice in Japanese culture, despite the fact that it has become secular, is probably much higher than that of the burek in Bosnian culture.

appear in naming. While the great majority of other ethnic communities from the former Socialist Federal Republic of Yugoslavia (SFRY) use the word burek to denote a dish made of phyllo dough filled with various meat, cheese, vegetable or fruit fillings, Bosnians are not so prone to burekgeneralizing. Bosnians, who more than any other group consider the burek to be their own, use the word burek to denote a dish made of phyllo dough filled (only) with meat. And it is one of a group of pies which includes "sirnica" (cheese filling), "krumpiruša" (potato), "zeljanica" (spinach), "kupuspita" (cabbage), "masiraca" (winter squash) "pita sa tikvom" (pumpkin), etc.[61] We could say that for the former, burek is an expression of form, while for the latter it is an expression of content.[62] Furthermore, bureks and other pies are indispensable elements of numerous religious, life and other events, Bosnian Muslim holidays (Bayram, weddings, etc.). But these are things which are outside the scope of this discussion. In immigrant families, the burek is not a commodity, it is inalienable: it is eaten by the people who made it or given to their family members and close friends. All participants in burekexchanges see it as a gift or as a mark of hospitality. The exchange of homemade bureks and on the other hand the production and consumption of industrial, bakery and street bureks indicate the difference between gift and commodity, as described in the more rigid social anthropology.[63] The relative separation and limited communication between

61 Even among pies there is a hierarchy, in which the meat burek (i.e., a "real" burek) is (clearly) the most highly valued. This is confirmed in the following Bosnian proverb: "Sve su pite pripitice, samo je pita burek(uša)—pita pitac!" [All pies are pies, but the burek is a pie among pies].

62 Bosnian burekinterpretation also prevailed in the first edition of the *Leksikon Yu mitologije* [Lexicon of Yugoslavian Mythology]: "For fabrications like 'apple burek,' offenders should be punished by having their food service licenses revoked." (Dejan Kršić, "Burek," in *Leksikon Yu mitologije* [Lexicon of Yugoslavian Mythology], ed. Iris Adrić *et al.* [Zagreb; Belgrade; Rende; Postscriptum, 2004], 65). In this narrow burekconception, Bosnia and Herzegovina is not an exception only in the area of the former SFRY, but in the Balkans in general, in Turkey and elsewhere. The broader appellation was probably introduced to Slovenia by the first burek stands, which are primarily run and staffed by Albanians from Macedonia (Martin Berishaj, conversation, 20 May 2005). It is however interesting that one can find several items in the Slovenian media in which this wider burekconception with respect to the narrower Bosnian understanding is recognized as a Slovenian specialty. They are interpreted either as a sort of cultural innovation or as ignorance with regard to recognizing and accepting other cultures.

63 These two economic systems developed at different levels of social development. The exchange of gifts is characteristic of clan-based societies, while market exchange is characteristic of class-based or state-based societies. Of course both forms of exchange coexist in complex state-based societies. As a "Slovene" example of this dialogue between gift and market exchange I can cite a

these two economies, or better, environments, is finally demonstrated by the fact that the great majority of immigrants mainly of the Muslim faith from the former SFRY who make bureks and other pies several times a week have never eaten a bakery-made or street burek during the entire time they have lived in Slovenia. On the other hand, I will also present a thesis on which I would bet my entire hard-earned fortune: if foreign burek stand and later domestic bakery and industrial burekproduction had not occurred, the majority of Slovenes would never even have heard of the burek. Or at least not in Slovenia.[64]

The burek's symbolic role is also different in various environments and economies. While in the market/commodity sphere the burek is above all a semioticized (symbolic) object, i.e. a sign for something,

---

highly original study by anthropologist Robert Minnich entitled "The Gift of Koline and the Articulation of Identity in Slovene Peasant Society," *Glasnik SED* 27, nos. 3–4 (1987): 171–179, which also helped me distinguish between the market and gift burek.

64 The exchange of homemade and non-homemade, i.e. made-for-market bureks, occurs along relatively narrowly delimited areas of economic exchange. In theory it is possible to exchange homemade bureks for money (whereby they become market goods), and to use non-homemade bureks as gifts or expressions of hospitality. But this probably happens very rarely.

The exchange of homemade bureks happens both inside and outside families, relations, and ethnic communities. Many immigrants often bring bureks and other pies for their co-workers at work, invite their friends, co-workers and acquaintances to their homes for bureks and other pies etc. In this context the exchange of bureks is an element of both separation and association at the same time. Why does a burek, like it or not, reflect a host's ethnic differentness, while its exchange establishes and maintains social connections? Burek gift-giving in Slovene society outlines the differences between the non-Slovene and the Slovene. But at the same time, like it or not, it also blurs them.

The conceptual and contextual difference between making and eating bureks and other pies in immigrant families and fast-food bureks is more than obvious. In the majority of immigrant families, bureks are prepared and eaten as the main daily meal, either for lunch or for dinner, and thus support the dominant traditional family meal structure. Street bureks most often resist this dominant meal structure. In immigrant families, bureks represent a relatively traditional element of nutrition, closely connected with the traditional culture, while fast-food bureks at least on city streets are kind of a newcomer, which Slovene cities and the majority of ethnic Slovenes have known for at most two or three decades. We could go on searching for differences, but that is not our primary preoccupation here.

These divisions are opposed by various new forms of burekmaking and burekeating. For example: the bureks made in certain "Slovene" bakeries, which are mainly sold in stores or bake shops. These bureks would be difficult to completely contain under the roof of the above stated definitions and divisions. They can be both an intrafamilal or an extrafamilal foodstuff, both a main dish or a different, non-conforming meal (a frozen burek, which is cooked at home and eaten for lunch or dinner—for instance together with a beef soup—or a burek bought in a store which is intended to be consumed immediately), or they could be something else entirely. Bureks made by "Slovene" families and individuals probably resist these divisions less. But these details and consistencies are once again outside the scope of this endeavour.

within the non-commodity sphere it is something more. Somewhat caricatured, so to speak, so that it not only reflects social relations, but also helps create them. Thus it is not just an object, but also, if I may be permitted to say so, a subject.

However, on the other hand it has to be said that these are not two entirely separate spheres. They are above all two conceptual and theoretical poles which in practice, in the real world of objects and material culture, are never completely realized, applied, or worked out, as modern theorists of material culture have shown.[65] As we will demonstrate below, people appropriate material culture in the commodity sphere; we appropriate things which are supposedly valued as commodities, and of course so-called gifts or, better, non-commodities never lie completely outside the range of commodity production.[66]

And in this discussion of the (non-)meeting of the immigrant and non-immigrant burek it is also not just that the line between gift and commodity is indistinct, blurred, and unclear, that things in their social lives move between different "regimes of value," as Arjun Appadurai said.[67] It is also that the rules from one apparently clearly delimited environment also extend into the space of the other, as we have already demonstrated with the making of less greasy, healthier bureks among immigrants and perhaps elsewhere as well. But let us return to the world of the "non-indigenous" burek and not abandon it, at least for

---

65 E.g. Arjun Appadurai, "Introduction: Commodities and the Politics of Value," in *The Social Life of Things: Commodities in Cultural Perspective*, ed. Arjun Appadurai (Cambridge: Cambridge University Press, 1992), 3–63; Daniel Miller, *Material Culture and Mass Consumption* (Oxford; New York: Blackwell, 1987).

66 However, a simple distinction between gifts and commodities—which was the basis for differentiating between communities defined by gift exchange and communities with commodity exchange—has to a great extent long been defined by the anthropological conceptualization and theoretization of material culture. Arjun Appadurai, Daniel Miller, and others, each with various approaches and concepts, have relativized this strict opposition. Anthropologists, says Miller in his study ("Artefacts and the Meaning of Things," in *Companion Encyclopedia of Anthropology*, ed. Tim Ingold [London; New York: Routledge, 1994], 396–419), exaggerated the totalitarian holism of smaller communities and in doing so usually ignored opposition and feelings of alienation, and on the other hand totally kept their eyes shut at home. They neglected the understanding of strategies through which people in industrial communities appropriated material culture. To loosely summarize Miller's warning: anthropologists found themselves in a silly, tragicomic situation in which they encountered a very small number of objects in the field which were mostly very important, while at home they were inundated with an unmanageably large number of objects whose importance was rarely worth mentioning.

67 Appadurai, "Introduction," 15.

some time. How quickly we can lose our way, and wander off on some life-altering tangent!

This traffic in meanings between the commodity and the non-commodity environments is in fact not a one-way street, as the reader might erroneously infer from the preceding example. The meaning and role of tradition—and the nutritional legitimacy of the burek also comes wrapped in this package—also appears outside of the immigrant milieu. But of course in a new space this tradition and meaning obtains new coordinates. The ObalaNET website, which represents three Slovene coastal communities (*obala* = coast), includes a page featuring the burek, where we read:

> *The burek is undoubtedly a dessert* with a tradition dating back a thousand years, *which has and will spread throughout the world with its unique flavour which makes the mouths of gourmets water, and I believe that their starving bellies will continue to be appeased by delicious bureks.*[68]

On a website which presents various views of the burek, on a subpage entitled "About the Burek," an anonymous author states the following:

> *The burek has been* among people for many years. *By this I do not mean to say just in Slovene society, but humanity, from its very beginnings. [...] It is not a fancy food like you can get at fancy hotels. The burek is not made following a precisely defined procedure; we are not talking about rigorous cuisine. It might be compared with impressionist painting. When you make a burek, you are left to your own initiative. Despite this, I have collected a few recipes which explain why homemade bureks are the best. If you are not exactly a talented chef, you can always go buy one. But it's interesting how bureks differ from kiosk to kiosk and bakery to bakery.*[69]

---

68 bosna_majka, accessed June 7, 2005, http://obala.net/index.php?show=news&action=news&id=9925&comments_perpage=13&comments_pa.

69 Anon., accessed August 2, 2007, http://web.s-gim.kr.edus.si/projekti/timko/2001_2002/burek-team/hpbbr/burek.htm.

Of course, this division is also considered in less economic/anthropological language. With a little help from Raymond Williams it could be said that bureks in immigrant families are a part of a sort of residual culture which is to a great extent removed from the dominant culture. But these residual meanings are to a great extent juxtaposed against opposing emergent meanings of the burek, particularly that part which is included in the dominant culture. On the conceptual level we therefore have two more or less opposing positions regarding the burek: unincorporated residual culture (the burek among immigrants) and incorporated emergent culture (the burek in healthy-lifestyle discourse).[70] So from here on—with these last examples, which honour the traditionality of the burek—the issue becomes even more complicated. We could say that the meanings and values from the residual culture are incorporated and recontextualized in the emergent culture, i.e. in that part of it which at least on some wider conceptual level stands in opposition to the dominant culture.

At any rate, the glorification of the traditionality of the burek—occasionally by emphasizing its links with the Balkans or the Orient[71]—and thus more or less the implicit consolidation of the burek's (nutritional) legitimacy, also seems to be a reflection of the mistrust for and dwindling reputation of modern systems of medical and nutritional knowledge and science. The appeal to tradition is itself the element that gives the burek legitimacy, some sort of established or confirmed quality in comparison with the ever-changing findings and instructions of nutritional, medical

---

70 Raymond Williams says the following on the difference between the residual and the emergent: "By 'residual' I mean that some experiences, meanings and values, which cannot be verified or cannot be expressed in terms of the dominant culture, are nevertheless lived and practiced on the basis of the residue—cultural as well as social—of some previous social formation." (Raymond Williams, "Base and Superstructure in Marxist Cultural Theory," *Culture and Materialism: Selected Essays* [London: Verso, 2005], 40) I should only add that despite its relative distance from the dominant culture, residual culture can be incorporated into it in concrete activities. "By 'emergent' I mean, first, that new meanings and values, new practices, new significances, and experiences, are continually being created. But there is a much earlier attempt to incorporate them, just because they are part—and yet not a defined part—of effective contemporary practice." (Williams, "Base and Superstructure," 41)

71 In this sense, i.e. a kind of glorification of traditional "Oriental" and/or "Balkan" food, such a statement could also be read as a "Western" discourse of power, in which the East represents in addition to a danger also a source of fascination. The wider framework of this debate is provided by Edward Said in *Orientalism* and Maria Todorova in *Imagining the Balkans*, which by analyzing "Western" conceptions of the Orient and the Balkans demonstrated that the latter occupies the place of the exotic Other in rational Europe. But more on this in the next chapter.

and other sciences. Discourse, which privileges the traditional, includes or at least is partially covered by the wider discursive system regarding naturalness, the fear of the "artificial," and doubts about the benefits of scientific progress. Pasi Falk thus finds that today's nutritional sphere is oriented to two bases: modernistic expert assessments, whose legitimacy is declining,[72] and on the other hand the premodern folk cultural tradition.[73] On one hand we therefore have various modernistic and medical discourses marked with scientific authority, and on the other hand discourse which draws its legitimacy from premodern folk tradition. Of course it is not necessary that there be an explicit, direct conflict between them. There could be a non-conflict-based cohabitation of otherwise conceptually opposing discourses which don't have much to agree on, as we might say in this particular case. At any rate, at least for the great majority of burekstatements which appeal to its traditionality, it would seem that there is no explicit strategy of undermining the dominant healthy-lifestyle discourse. We therefore have to deal with an implicit, alternative discourse which draws its meanings, values and value from some residual culture or remains, and which is significantly less motivated, engaged and articulated than the dominant science-sanctified discourse.

Of course, on some wider semantic level, the attitude of this modernistic healthy-lifestyle discourse towards the burek is opposed by all approbatory, affirmative, positive burekstatements—in short, statements that confirm the legitimacy of the burek in their own ways, in different directions and with very different approaches. They do this most often quite indirectly, unnoticeably and unintentionally, for instance through the publication of numerous burekrecipes both online and in print and other media, in articles and other journalism which touch on

72 There are of course several reasons for the diminishing reputation of nutritional and other sciences associated with healthy-lifestyle discourse. One of the more problematic consequences of the scope of nutritional science and also one of the reasons for its diminishing reputation is the pronounced lack of transparency and contradictoriness of the various reports, advice and findings on what is or is not healthy. The consequence is not just a loss of reputation for (nutritional) science, but undoubtedly also an increasing level of distrust at the level of everyday life.

73 See Pasi Falk, *The Consuming Body.* Norman Fairclough notes that the dominant discourse in the area of healthy lifestyle practices today is "medical discourse," which at the same time is faced with the contrasting positions of "alternative discourses" (e.g. acupuncture, homeopathy) and so-called folk discourses. (*Discourse and Social Change* [Cambridge; Oxford: Polity Press; Blackwell, 1992], 3)

the burek in one way or another, in portraits of well-known personalities who admit that they eat or make bureks, or by assessing the quality of bureks. Let's have a look at just a few of the enormous number of such not particularly or not at all engaged or motivated statements.

We very often find highly favourable descriptions and mentions of bureks in various travelogues from foreign countries (Bosnia and Herzegovina, Macedonia, Albania, Turkey, Greece, etc.). In an article on Bosnia and Herzegovina we read:

> *You can't leave Baščaršija [the old town centre of Sarjevo] without trying a burek. Their "burekžinice" [traditional burek shops] are lined up one after the other. The selection is huge. We decided to try a cabbage and a classic cheese. [...] The cheese burek was truly fantastic, the cabbage a little less so, as it has a very strong flavour, which you either enjoy or not.*[74]

Sometimes the title of the article tells you everything, as in the title of a travelogue on Albania: "Thank Goodness You Can Get a Burek Anywhere."[75] And of course bureks appear in other forms of journalism, for instance in a sort of combination of reporting and feature writing on the work of the Operational Communications Centre in Ljubljana (i.e. the emergency call line, telephone number 113) and the work of the police night shift entitled "One, One, Three, Burek at Midnight" (it both scans and rhymes in Slovene), where we read:

> *And while we are talking about employment, comparisons and Canadians: while the latter as devotees of North American police folklore are most likely to graze on boring old doughnuts, the Ljubljana squad refresh themselves with a midnight burek, and they of course send the youngest officer to buy them.*[76]

---

74 Simona Novak, "Mesto, ki je ohranilo dušo" [The Town which Kept Its Soul], *Delo*, August 10, 2005, 17.

75 Gorazd Šajn, "Še dobro, da se povsod dobi burek" [Thank Goodness You Can Get a Burek Anywhere], *Dnevnik*, July 23, 2003, 24.

76 Borut Mehle, "Ena, ena, tri—burek ob polnoči" [One, One, Three, Burek at Midnight], *Dnevnik*, December 23, 1999, 16.

So, boring doughnuts and refreshing bureks!

Recipes, on the other hand, form a specific, complex field of consolidation of the status and legitimacy—and, as we will see in the following story, also the repudiation and exclusion—of the burek. There is a huge number of burekrecipes on various websites dedicated to cooking. On what is probably Slovenia's main culinary portal, "Kulinarična Slovenija" [Culinary Slovenia], there are a full 24,[77] for example:

77 See Kulinarika.net, accessed May 28, 2008, http://www.kulinarika.net/baze/receptirezultati.asp?besede=burek.

BUREK *

Ingredients: 1 lb. pastry flour, 2 Tbs. oil, lukewarm water (as needed), salt. **Filling:** 13 oz. ground beef, 3 Tbs. lard, 2 onions chopped in a meat grinder, salt and pepper to taste, 3 eggs.

Make a smooth soft dough and pound it on the table. My mother would throw it in the air 30 times and smack it on the counter. This makes the dough elastic. Then shape it into a ball, coat it with oil to keep it from drying out and cover it with a warm dish. Let it stand at least one hour. Then you will be able to stretch it out without making holes. Of course this takes a lot of practice. Some people then cut the stretched crust of dough and cook them on the stove. In order to have a good burek you have to use real lard instead of oil, or at least half and half. Fry the onion in oil, add meat and cover until all of the liquid is cooked off. Add salt and pepper. Cool the meat. Add beaten eggs to the cooled meat and you have filling for a meat burek. To make a cheese burek, take non-lowfat cheese, add a little mineral water or other water, salt and pepper. Some people also add cream. Grease a baking sheet with a layer of lard or oil, cover it with one layer of dough and sprinkle with hot lard. Then add the second layer of dough and sprinkle again. Add the filling over the third layer, and then dough and filling until you have used all your filling. The last layer has to be dough, which also gets sprinkled with lard. Bake in a very hot oven. When done, sprinkle with water and cover with a kitchen towel. Then it is ready to cut.

* Marinka, accessed July 17, 2008, http://www.kulinarika.net/recept.asp?ID=105

BUREK[**]

Dough: 10 oz. pastry flour, salt, ½ cup oil, a little warm water.

Filling: meat, potatoes, onions, spices.

The filling can be meat, cheese or a combination.

For the filling prepare the ground meat to your taste. Dice 4 or 5 potatoes into small cubes. Slice one white and one red onion similarly finely. Add a little oil, Vegeta, pepper, a good amount of salt, ground paprika and garlic. Mix.

Instructions: Spread a tablecloth on the table. Roll the dough out thin. Wrap it around a rolling pin in order to stretch it. Then coat with oil. Fold the edges towards the centre of the dough so that the edges get oiled as well and fold back. Let the dough stand at room temperature for 15 minutes so that it rests. Then stretch well with your hands across the entire table, very thin. Spread the filling along the edge of the dough, in a 4-inch wide strip. Start rolling the edges by lifting the tablecloth. Meanwhile, pull the burek towards you several times, so that the dough in the middle stretches and thins. Soon the dough in the middle will tear; wrap the burek completely. The burek is now in the shape of a continuous ring around the entire table. Cut it into long sections and roll them into a circle like a snake. Place the bureks onto a greased baking sheet. Coat them with oil or even better with pieces of butter, which will melt during baking. Bake at 480°F until it turns reddish-brown. Towards the end sprinkle it with water (a spray bottle works best) and bake a little longer. When done, spread a little cream on them, either neutral or sour cream, never sweet!

Bon appetit!

These bureks were made by my friend Emina from Bosnia.

** Ales6m, accessed May 28, 2008, http://www.kulinarika.net/recept.asp?ID=3337

"SIRNICA" CHEESE PIE ***

(Better known in Slovenia as a cheese burek. This is more of a southern recipe, but is also prepared farther north – for example in Niš in Serbia.)

Dough: 1 lb. pastry flour, approx. 1–1¼ cups lukewarm water, 1 Tbs. vinegar, a couple of pinches of salt, 3 heaping Tbs. lard, approx. ½ cup oil.
Filling: 1–1¼ lbs. cottage cheese (nonfat), 1–2 tsp. salt (to taste), 1–2 Tbs. sour cream (as needed).

Mix the dough ingredients and knead well until it becomes smooth and soft (10–15 minutes). Divide it into 5 or more balls and roll each one into a circle approx. 4"–6" in diameter. Mix the melted lard and oil and set the rolled out pieces of dough into the mixture. Let stand for around 10 minutes. Take a piece of dough out of the oil and lard mixture and place it on a smooth work surface (the best place is a large table, which can be protected with a smooth plastic tablecloth). Stretch the dough by hand into as large a circle as possible, then lift the edge of the dough and using your hands slowly stretch it towards you from the centre from all sides until thin. Cut away any remaining thick edges. Try to avoid making holes, but it's okay if there are some. Mix the ingredients for the filling and sprinkle some of it over the stretched dough. Fold the edges of the dough towards the centre (it can be folded several times) and set aside. Repeat with the remaining three pieces of dough, but save at least one for the end. Stretch the last piece of dough, lightly sprinkle it with filling and set the stretched, filled and folded pieces next to each other in the centre. Add more filling as needed and fold the edges of the dough across all of the pieces so that they are closed into the burek. Carefully, so that the dough does not break, transfer the entire burek into a round baking tray and bake at 400°F for 45–50 minutes until golden brown.

This method of making phyllo dough is fairly simple, but the result is very tasty. Since the dough is evenly and well-greased, it sticks to

*** Grunf, accessed May 28, 2008, http://www.kulinarika.net/recept.asp?ID=10675.

smooth surfaces and can be stretched thinly quite easily. I strongly recommend using lard (either mixed with oil or just pure lard), since at the end the dough is nicely crunchy and tastier. In Bosnia they stretch their phyllo dough "dry" (without a lot of grease) and bake it nearly dry right on the stovetop, and while preparing the burek sprinkle it generously with a decoction of water and lard. This dough can be made in advance and stored similarly to the phyllo dough that can be purchased in stores. The pictures show the final product and the final stage of preparation—when the last piece of dough has been stretched, with four turnovers in the background waiting to be folded into the final piece of dough.

KROMPIRUŠA (POTATO STRUDEL) ****

(Quick recipe)

Burek dough: 2 lbs. potatoes, 1 onion, 2 cloves of garlic, pepper, 4 Tbs. sour cream (or milk), butter or oil as needed

Peel and wash the potatoes and dice into cubes or grate coarsely. Fry a finely-chopped onion in oil until it begins to caramelize, add potatoes, pepper, a little Vegeta, salt and fry lightly, for about 10 minutes. Then separate the dough sheet by sheet, sprinkle them with oil, spread the potato preparation on them and fold them into turnovers.

Place a turnover at the centre of an oiled baking tray and fold it into a circle. Wrap the next sheet around the last and so on. Bake in an oven at 350°F for 30 minutes, before the baking is completed, cover with sour cream (or sour milk or ordinary milk) and at the end coat with lard.

**** Bgajo, accessed May 28, 2008, http://www.kulinarika.net/recept.asp?ID=4599.

While the website of the "Društvo dobrih okusov Gurman" ['Gourmet' Good Tastes Association], which does not exactly appear to be a plebeian organization, only has a recipe for a cheese burek.[78] Here and there you can find burekrecipes on websites which have nothing to do with cooking, for instance on the abovementioned website which presents "various views" of the burek,[79] or in more minimalistic forms on numerous chat rooms such as "Lunin Forum."[80] You can also find several recipes in print media,[81] both "classical" (e.g. a recipe for meat burek among recipes by master chef Janez Štrukelj in a column in the newspaper *Večer* entitled "Wine, Cuisine, and Beauty,"[82] and various offshoots, e.g. the "Euroburek" (spinach, meat and cheese),[83] "a little more SLO and veggie, and mushrooms for a change."[84] After looking through dozens of cookbooks—i.e. books, undoubtedly a more selective and controlled environment—I only managed to find burekrecipes in the general *Kuhinja naše družine* [Our Family Cuisine] [85] and the thematic *Kuhinje Balkana: Razkošje okusov za vse priložnosti* [Cuisines of the Balkans: Luxury of Tastes for all Occasions].[86] But let's talk about the disparity between the wealth to be found on the profane websites and the paucity of the world of books in the next chapter.

To conclude these politically unmotivated, unengaged statements, let's have a look at celebrities. Slovene pop-singer Saška Lendero in an article in the tabloid *Nova* magazine entitled "After the EMAs She Went Out for a Burek" she says that after performing at the show at which the Slovenian entry in the Eurovision Song Contest is chosen:

---

78 Anon., accessed August 2, 2007, http://www.gurman.eu/recipes.php?S=6&Article=699.

79 Anon., accessed August 2, 2007, http://web.s-gim.kr.edus.si/projekti/timko/2001_2002/burekteam/hpbbr/recepti.htm (2 August 2007).

80 Tamara, accessed August 2, 2007, http://www.lunin.net/forum/index.php?showtopic=1358&hl=-burek.

81 The first written burekrecipe I found in Slovene was in the newspaper *Večer* from 1963 (see Anon., "Jutri na mizi" [On the Table Tomorrow], *Večer*, March 6, 1963, 4).

82 Anon., "Recepti Janeza Štruklja" [The Recipes of Janez Štrukelj], *Večer*, August 9, 2001, 34.

83 Matevž Šalehar, "Prvi Evrogrižljaj" [The First Eurosnack], *Večer*, May 7, 2004, 57.

84 Matevž Šalehar, "Da burek ne bo Turek" [So that the Burek won't be Turkish], *Večer*, January 23, 2004, 57.

85 Stanko Grafenauer, *Kuhinja naše družine* [Our Family Cuisine] (Ljubljana: Mladinska knjiga, 2002), 195–196.

86 Radojko Mrlješ et al., *Kuhinje Balkana: Razkošje okusov za vse priložnosti* [Cuisines of the Balkans: Luxury of Tastes for all Occasions] (Tržič: Učila International, 2005).

> *I had to do interviews until 12:30 in the morning, and then Miha and I went to Nobel Burek. Since a lot of friends said they were coming over, we bought two whole boxes of bureks. (Laughs) Of course we had a serious talk at home with our friends afterwards, a real burek party, since we were all hungry[.]*[87]

The same story was also published in the tabloid *Slovenkse novice* in an article with the title "Saška's Burek: Everyone's favourite pop singer swallows her sorrows after her (un)professional appearance at the EMAs."[88] I could also list various statements by foreigners living in Slovenia. When Mormon missionary Jordan Cullimore was asked in *Jana* magazine about Slovenia's culinary highlights, he answered "I'm going to miss Cockta [Slovenia's version of Coca-Cola], bureks and Poli salami when I leave."[89]

However, approving, affirmative conceptualizations of the burek are not formed only in language statements, but also in production, consumption, etc. With a considerable amount of abstraction and probably also uncriticalness, we could even say that every well-made burek eaten with satisfaction consolidates bureklegitimacy, although much less obviously than for instance the more visible representations of the burek in the media and popular culture.

In this discussion of the affirmation, inclusion and domestication of the burek, we must not forget about certain contextual, physical-environmental changes that the burek has undergone in the past twenty years. The burek's move and expansion from its classical production and consumption environment in Slovenia (immigrant families and fast-food joints) into new environments ("Slovene" bakeries and industrial food processing plants and "Slovene" households/individuals) seems to have brought the burek a significant amount of nutritional legitimacy, a complex and multivarious legitimacy which I will not take the time to dissect here. But I should mention the burek being made and sold

87 Marjanca Likovič, "Po Emi odšla na burek" [After the EMAs She Went Out for a Burek], *Nova*, February 20, 2006, 40–41.

88 A. Z., "Saškin burek" [Saška's Burek], *Slovenske novice*, February 1, 2006, 12.

89 Anon., "Izjave tedna" [Quotes of the Week], *Slovenske novice*, February 1, 2006, 12.

in so-called "ethnic" restaurants, e.g. Turkish (Yildiz Han in Ljubljana, once under the same name in Koper), Bosnian (Sofra, Deset v pol, partially at Sofrica, all in Ljubljana), Miraz (Maribor and elsewhere), Greek (the former Atene restaurant in Ljubljana), in ethnically difficult to define or ethnically hybrid restaurants (e.g. the restaurant Aska in volk in Ljubljana which features the cuisine of the Balkans and the countries of the former SFRY, as evidenced by its very name—"Aska and the Wolf," a fairy tale written by Ivo Andrić—and particularly by its menu, in which we find burek listed as "Serbian gibanica"), etc. In these restaurants the patrons eat dishes which they usually see on the street as fast food, in a totally new, higher-status role, often also under different names, which probably also adds to the surprise. In this context it is also not insignificant that the status of ethnic food and ethnic restaurants at least in certain social environments is increasing, as evidenced by the growth of supposedly higher quality, more expensive restaurants serving ethnic food. But these are other questions, which hang awkwardly—like excess on the edges—from this nicely stretched dough.

The burek receives further confirmation of this approving attitude, this affirmative discourse, from statements by well-known personalities who are prepared to expose their skill at making bureks to the general public. This articulation of production and media representations is probably most frequent in the print media. TV presenter Saša Einsiedler e.g. gives us a recipe in *Nedelo* for "savoury pie for meat-eaters," where she "took a classical recipe for burek and added her own touches."[90] And when an anonymous reporter for *Pilot* asks her what kind of dish she would cook for him/her, she once again speaks only of "meat pie à la Saša," which originated in an attempt to make a burek.[91] The same could be said about consumption: consumption and representation are probably more commonly reflected in admissions, emphasis and disclosure of a star's enjoyment of bureks. Just remember "Saška's burek," where "everyone's favourite pop singer swallow[ed] her sorrows after her (un)professional appearance at the EMAs."[92]

90 Miko Klavdija, "Začinjena pita za mesojedce" [Savory Pie for Meat-Eaters], *Ona*, February 3, 2004, 55.
91 Anon., "Imejmo se radi" [Let's Love Each Other], *Pilot*, March 27, 2005.
92 A. Z., "Saškin burek."

As an example of the signifying practices, the statements which form within the general field of consumer and media representations and in the final analysis production as well, we can also list parties, events, film premieres, comic strips, etc., in which the burek figures particularly prominently. But more on that in the next chapter.

Undoubtedly such a narrow reading of these apparently well-intentioned burekstatements could be highly problematic. Nearly all of the statements cited in this subchapter, from "Saška's burek" to the expansion of burekproduction in supposedly well-regarded restaurants and industrial food processing companies could be speaking about a hidden process which Dick Hebdige designated incorporation or inclusion.[93] This, as Hebdige finds, occurs on two levels, through two processes: (a) through the conversion of alternative or oppositional signifiers—i.e. signifiers which stand in opposition to the dominant culture—into products of mass production, which Hebdige called the commodity form, and (b) through the labelling and redefining by dominant groups of the practices, styles, behaviours and objects which the dominant culture finds disturbing so that they fit into their conceptual frameworks (what Hebdige calls the ideological form).[94]

After this intrusion by Hebdige, a question arises in a loud voice: are these well-meaning, affirmative, inclusive, positive, friendly, appreciative burekstatements nothing but a way of avoiding the possibility that the burek is a threat to our existence?

Before we attempt to answer this question, let's have a look at those reformers who are clearly doing the opposite of the inclusion described above, who tend to impose alternative or oppositional meanings onto things loaded with the meanings of the dominant culture. Actually, we could also speak of inclusion with regard to these oppositional or alternative practices,[95] except that it happens in the opposite direction: from

93 Hebdige, *Subculture*, 94. Hebdige uses the concept of incorporation in an analysis of British postwar subcultural styles. In Hebdige's case the so-called commodity forms are subcultural signals (clothes, music), and the ideological forms are primarily the deviant behaviour of the subculture groups.

94 For more on the incorporation of practices into the dominant culture cf. Williams' abovementioned "Base and Superstructure."

95 For more on the difference between oppositional and alternative, see the following chapter.

the dominant to the oppositional culture. So who are these topplers, these modifiers, nonconformists of meaning, these...

...Burekwarriors?

Food, especially fast food, is one of the great battlefields,[96] where battles rage between parents and children, old and young. Numerous studies have shown that children and teenagers often use food in order to establish their personal autonomy and as a means of rebellion against the authority of adults.[97] On the other side, that of the parents, nutrition and diet is one of the most important fields in which the authority of parents and adults can be established. Of course, this doesn't always work out so well for them:

> *If for schoolchildren (I'm swallowing all of my pride here) yesterday was more a day of mourning for the holidays than joy for the opening of the school doors, some were looking towards the school doors eagerly. For them the beginning of classes is also a holiday, as it brings an exceptional amount of income. Yesterday, the sandwich generations filled the small bakeries, where they fill their bellies with bureks, sandwiches, rolls, pizzas, and everything else our youth eats with gusto throughout the school year. Even more thrilled were the owners of all of the million little cafés near (most of all secondary) schools, where the hordes of youth take over the tables and chairs. [...] Long live the first day of school, the holiday of fast food and cafés!*[98]

---

96 To give just one example of a more explicit modern regulation of fast food to be found in the daily newspaper: Mahmoud Ahmadinejad, the conservative President of Iran, ordered the closing of fast food restaurants and prohibited billboards with David Beckham's image (see Barbara Šurk, "Mahmud Ahmadinežad" [Mahmoud Ahmadinejad], *Delo, Sobotna priloga*, July 2, 2005, 3).

97 See Lupton, *Food, the Body and the Self*, 55–59. This includes an affinity for fast food, vegetarianism and eating disorders. Adolescent girls and young women in particular, in Lupton's opinion use food to express disagreement or rebellion, since they have fewer social resources at their disposal than men do.

98 n. n., "Praznik" [Holiday], *Dnevnik*, September 2, 2004, 32.

The above example shows that food divides parents and children on several levels. In addition to the disciplining of children and young people we can also see the special status of young people's food in nutritional ideology. As various studies have shown, children's favourite foods have relatively low nutritional status.[99] The same could probably be said about the favourite dishes and foods of children in Slovenia, which, as indicated not only by the youth but also by the just as numerous statements, includes the burek. In an article entitled "Signs that You're an Adult..." in the newspaper *Večer*, one of the signs of adulthood is that "[Y]ou don't know the price of a burek or the price of a beer at the coolest place in town[.]"[100]

Let's return to disciplining the youth and their avoidance and opposition to it, and to eating bureks. As was made clear in conversations with secondary-school students, groups of boys, primarily or exclusively from gymnasiums (i.e. college preparatory schools for the students with the highest aptitude), employ symbolic consumption, a studied ingesting of greasy bureks, as a form of rebellion against the dominant healthy-lifestyle discourse with which they are bombarded in the media, advertising, formal and informal education.[101] Healthy lifestyle discourse is wary of the burek, and views it defensively with a double perspective: it threatens the "*strejt*" (i.e. "straight") world (and is therefore suspicious), and it is a signifier of a forbidden identity.

For these students, primarily or exclusively groups of boys, not all bureks are equally good. The only good or real burek is a greasy burek made and sold on the city streets, usually only by certain Albanian burekmakers. Bureks which are considered to be less greasy, i.e. those produced by "Slovene" bakeries and industrial firms, are not considered good bureks. The ideal burek is therefore, as one can hear among secondary-schoolers, an "ultragreasy burek," where the "grease runs

99 See Blanka Tivadar, "Hrana kot simbolna potrošnja" [Food as Symbolic Consumption] (PhD diss., University of Ljubljana, 1998), 57.

100 Anon., "Znaki, da ste odrasli...." [Signs that You're an Adult...], *Večer*, July 11, 2002, 36.

101 A study of the eating habits of Ljubljana eighth graders showed that "eighth graders are well acquainted with healthy lifestyles and nutrition and that fast food is not considered healthy food" (Meta Medved et al., "Prehrambne navade ljubljanskih osmošolcev" [The Nutritional Habits of Ljubljana Eighth-Graders], *Zdravstveno varstvo* 37 (1998): 312.

through the paper." Anže Jesenko, a student at the Škofja Loka classical gymnasium, who admits to making fun, burek in hand, of losing weight and counting calories, says in an email "that a greasy burek is usually better... when you get a burek that you can see through the paper, you already know it's going to be good[.]"[102] Bežigrad Gymnasium student Jure Vogrinc is even more emphatic: "The definition of a burek is that it has to be greasy."[103] But direct statements are not the only way that this subversiveness of eating bureks is communicated. Eating bureks is frequently seasoned with jokes about counting calories, obesity, women's avoidance of fatty foods and nutritious foods in general, and about health. I will list just a few of these statements served up by the bursting-with-ideas Jure Vogrinc, and some which I overheard while observing a small group of secondary-school students eating bureks one day in the spring of 2007 in front of the Dino Burek snack bar at the entrance to the Plava Laguna (Blue Lagoon) shopping centre in Ljubljana: "Hey, let's count calories!"; "One time my friend asked [a burek seller] for a diet burek. I have no idea whether he understood."; "'I'm not going to have a whole burek; let's just buy one.' And there are five of us (laughter). Two or three girls take one between them. I took two for myself."; "These greasy bureks (from a street burekvendor) aren't healthy. Let's go to McDonald's, it's healthier."; "I can't have bureks; I'll get fat."[104]

A group of students from the Bežigrad Gymnasium who occasionally exchange their school lunch for a burek or go to a nearby burekjoint after a difficult, tiring, stultifying class, often make jokes at the expense of the clerk who works there. They say she only washes her hands only once a week, and this lack of hygiene is supposed to be the key to the greasiness of the burek. If she washes her hands on Thursday evening, the bureks will be less greasy on Friday morning, but will become greasier and greasier each following day.[105]

Fat, that demonic substance, that cornerstone of offence, at least in the more fictive segment of healthy-lifestyle discourse, becomes

102 Anže Jesenko, e-mail message to author, March 21, 2005.

103 Jure Vogrinc, conversation, July 7, 2006.

104 Vogrinc, conversation, July 7, 2006, and participant observation.

105 Vogrinc, conversation, July 7, 2006.

among secondary-school students a quality about which they yell at the top of their lungs. Of course in this story, at least in my opinion, the starring role is played by the burek. And not just because of its proverbial greasiness and frequent association with healthy-lifestyle discourse, but also or even primarily because of the popularity—the accessibility and filling quality—of the burek. But let's start this story from a slightly different angle.

It seems that power relations are not without places of disobedience. But disobedience and rebellion, as the above-cited Dick Hebdige and others have pointed out, are carried out and manifested at the level of everyday, apparently banal and unimportant things.[106] They are not necessarily reflected and do not necessarily occur in direct opposition in the form of some great ideas. In the case of secondary-school students eating bureks this rebellion seems somewhat more grounded and materialized. What do I mean by this? I mean that this teenage rebellion cannot be primarily understood as opposition to the hegemonic ideas of healthy-lifestyle discourse, in which the burek is merely a medium, a semiotic weapon, a signifier. I believe that this has to be understood more as a rebellion with the burek and for the burek, and not as a clear and planned rebellion against the dominant healthy-lifestyle discourse. Healthy-lifestyle discourse thus appears as an appendage, a parasite on the popular, cheap, available almost anywhere anytime and filling burek, which gives further meaning and nuance to this rebellion with/for the burek. This is also borne witness to by conversations with burekwarriors, who only rarely and with difficulty are able to perceive, recognize or conceptualize the alleged major enemy—healthy-lifestyle discourse. Miha Čančula, a friend and schoolmate of the author of the majority of the above statements, Jure Vogrinc, makes the following comment on his friend's joking and his own loyalty to the burek:

---

106 Dick Hebdige, in his analysis of British subcultures after the Second World War in his book *Subculture*, shows that the subculture's challenge to the dominant culture does not originate directly through their opposition to it, and in fact is not merely reflected but also occurs mainly at the level of style.

> *Yeah, Jure loves to say those kinds of things. And then we crack up. But at least in my case it's usually more about making fun of girls who really think they're fat and that they have to lose weight and all. But it's also because bureks are good. I never even thought about a rebellion against the media because I usually don't read that kind of stuff and even when I do, it doesn't interest me.*[107]

Therefore, as we have said above, for the dominant discourse the burek is a signifier of a forbidden identity, threatens the dominant worldview, and in this battle for the burek some burekwarriors—but by no means all—more or less consciously also recognize the burek's enemy, which due to its omnipresence, its close association with girls' obsession with thinness and having a beautiful body and probably other things as well, it seems to be a particularly handy, fun and beloved enemy. And of course it seems that for all of this, jokes, wisecracks and fun are more important than any serious rebellion, great ideas or objectives.

As Dick Hebdige has shown, a subculture cannot be understood as a direct revolt against the dominant culture, hegemony and consensus that those in power have enforced. The rebellion occurs through a spectacular style, which has to be understood, says Hebdige, as intentional communication—communication which is emphasized and unusual within the subcultures, which attracts attention, which represents, overthrows and destroys the dominant meaning and uses of commodities.[108] But of course this intentional communication—at least in the case of teenagers eating bureks—has to be read as intentional at the level of the subculture. And this in no way means that it is done consciously or is even understood by all of the individuals in the subculture.

In unravelling the appropriation of the burek by secondary-school students, we now must search for the beginning of the story in the

107 Miha Čančula, e-mail message to author, July 13, 2006.

108 Among British subcultural styles, at least in Hebdige's time, this recontextualization of commodities and objects was most clearly expressed and in the clothing style of the punk rockers. Objects from the most banal contexts—WC chains, safety pins, plastic bags, tampons, razor blades—became a part of their style. (Hebdige, *Subculture*, 107 sq.)

burek's accessibility, affordability and being filling. Only then do the meanings, discourses and rebellions which flavour the consumption and appropriation appear.

We can also detect subversiveness or at least a certain ironic stance towards the hegemonic healthy-lifestyle discourse, of course in the context of the burek and its unhealthiness and greasiness, outside of the context of secondary-school students. A renowned judge of bureks who has already been cited several times has this to say about the zucchini burek from the Damajanty Seam bakery in Ljubljana:

> *[T]o determine whether the non-greasy vegetable filling or the burek stand and the global horizons of the main burekbaker are responsible for the dryness. [...] The vicinity of the hospital gives the burek stand a whiff of health or at least of heath safety... which in my opinion is also the main culprit for the non-greasiness of the bureks.*[109]

Screenwriter Tomaž Cuder, in a column entitled "Before Deletion" in the Saturday Supplement to the newspaper *Večer*, which features statements by more or less well-known figures, says: "A dream woman does not need fitness or aerobics, she eats bureks, knows how to change a tire and doesn't use the lame old excuse that she has a headache."[110] To put it in the weighty words of Michel Foucault, "For, if it is true that at the heart of power relations and as a permanent condition of their existence there is an insubordination and a certain essential obstinacy on the part of the principles of freedom, then there is no relationship of power without the means of escape or possible flight."[111]

Let's return from these lofty words for a moment to young people and their eating of bureks. It has to be said that the symbolic consumption of bureks by secondary-school students and youths also

---

109 Franc Marušič, accesssed Autumn, 2006, http://www.delo.si/blog/ivanmars/index.php?BLOG_PATH=220&BLOG_ARCHIVE.

110 Tomaž Cuder, "Pred izbrisom" [Before Deletion], *Večer, Sobotna priloga*, April 23, 2005, 34.

111 Foucault, "The Subject and Power," 225.

incorporates other aspects of rebellion. As stated above, secondary-school students and youths eating bureks is mostly about rebellion with the burek and for the burek, which has to be understood as a sort of catch-all of various meanings, interests and associations. However, it is also or even mostly about rebellion against Americanization, which is very often symbolized by "McDonald'sization" (as evidenced by several online debates, and even the title of the thread "Burek vs. McDonald's" and of course the content of this debate on the website of the Slovenian Tolkien Association Gil-galad),[112] about the opposition to the dominant family meal structure and rebellion against adult authority in general, about rejecting "Yugophobia", "Balkanophobia" and other nationalistic phenomena (which manifest themselves in debates, comments and statements on numerous websites and chat rooms—for instance the text entitled "Yes to bureks but no to mosques, eh?" on the "Student Info" website, the site of a hotly contested debate).[113] A great deal of these symbolic meanings of the burek among secondary-school students and young people in general can also be found in the wide variety of (sub)cultural productions: in many different types of forms on websites, in jokes, wisecracks, stories, etc.[114] What do you think this scrawl means?

---

112 Zygo, accessed August 2, 2007, http://www.gil-galad.info/smf/index.php?topic=213.0.

113 Sandra Prajnić, accessed July 13, 2006, http://www.student-info.net/portal/portal.php?stran=prva&vs=novice&id=173. The same text with the same title can also be found elsewhere, for instance at the beginning of one of the debates on the ObalaNET website.

114 The lyrics to the song *B mashina* by the rock group Siddharta were transformed by Bežigrad Gymnasium student Miha Čančula into "Burek Mashina" (i.e. Burek Machine) (Miha Čančula, accessed August 27, 2007, http://www.geocities.com/metalec_mobitela/fore/BMashina.doc). He also wrote a poem when his favourite "burekaš" at the Emona station closed his burek stand (the poem was unfortunately never written down) (Miha Čančula, e-mail message to author, July 12, 2006). Jure Vogrinc reports that the following joke occurs frequently in his class: "Let's say there is some new concept and people don't know how to pronounce it, *eventually* or *evantually*. Then somebody in the class says 'E as in burek.'" That is, any letter as in burek. When they go for a burek with their classmates or friends, they often invent new jokes or wisecracks relating to the burek and repeat old ones, such as: "Let's go make a fish burek." (Jure Vogrinc, conversation, July 7, 2006). Even a quick glance into the past gives us an insight into the wealth of secondary-school or youth burekprodution. In the mid-nineties there were dozens of so-called garage (hardcore, punk, ska) bands with lyrics in which the burek appeared in one way or another. Poljane Gymnasium student Ivan Mitrevski (conversation, summer, 2005) e.g. remembers a group from the mid-nineties called *Kripel Bataljon* [i.e. Cripple Battalion] with a song or a chorus to a song that went "Burek, burek, oy, oy, oy."

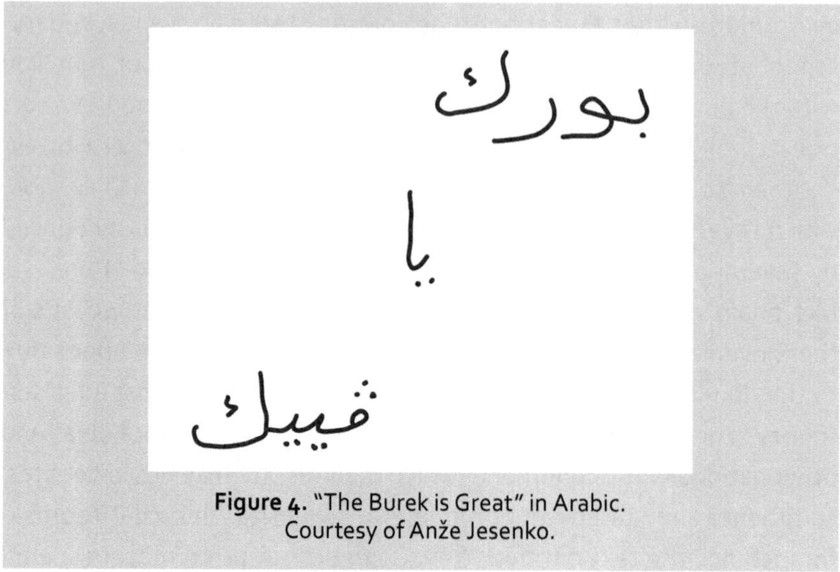

Figure 4. "The Burek is Great" in Arabic.
Courtesy of Anže Jesenko.

It is an inscription of "The Burek is Great" in Arabic, a paraphrase of "God/Allah is great," which is displayed on the home page of the website of a student at the Škofija Classical Gymnasium. On the minimalist home page he also presents a distich, a paraphrase of a famous poem known to all Slovenes, by Slovenia's most famous poet, France Prešeren:

The women of Ljubljana were long renowned for their beauty
But none were better than a meaty [burek][115]

He also named his server after a burek. His email address is therefore: mesni@burek.uni.cc (i.e. meat@burek.uni.cc). He says: "Some (people who visited his website and enjoyed it) have asked me for an email address on my server, and of course they got them. Having a burek address is a real status symbol."[116] In response to my question "Why burek?" he replies in a Zen-like manner: "maybe because I like to eat bureks :)."[117]

115 Anže Jesenko, accessed August 16, 2006, http://burek.uni.cc/.
116 Jesenko, e-mail message to author, March 22, 2005.
117 Jesenko, e-mail message to author, March 21, 2005.

Slovenes into Europe with Bureks and/or the Dictatorship of the Carniolan Sausage, and most of all a good joke: on the burek and the national essence

The Dictatorship of the Carniolan Sausage

The title of this section is taken from the hegemonic Slovenian newspaper *Delo*. This commentary, the title of which is wreathed in Carniolan sausage (*kranjska klobasa*—Slovenia's central culinary symbol, the standard-bearer of Slovenian cuisine), refers primarily to European integration processes, and also includes the following:

> *Slovenes fortunately eat Carniolan sausage, at least that is what we hear, and these days some anti-national fanatics have even put on some kind of public protest against the 'dictatorship of the Carniolan sausage.' This is nice to hear, as the conventional wisdom is hinting at a dictatorship of the burek and čevapčiči.*[118]

It therefore ostensibly refers to dictatorship or dictatorships, those fear-mongering political systems which I will dwell on only in reference to the marketing-style title. And also in sentences of more literary, free-spirited provenience with which I will try to loosen up the text, and even perhaps laugh in the midst of all this scientific gravity. But how did we get to these alleged dictatorships or the idea of dictatorships of such well-meaning things as Carniolan sausage, čevapčiči, and bureks?

In 1982, Bojan Štih published a daily column titled "That's Not a Poem, That's Just Love" in the most popular Slovenian cultural and intellectual journal *Naši razgledi* [Our Viewpoints], which sparked a huge controversy which exceeded the scope of the discussion in question. It seems, if I may be allowed to indulge in a bit of literary prose, that this well-known essayist, critic, theatre director, playwright, etc., opened a bottle that was by

118 Boris Jež, "Diktatura kranjske klobase" [The Dictatorship of the Carniolan Sausage], *Delo, Sobotna priloga*, February 28, 2004, 4.

no means empty. And the genie of course wanted out. But what kind of genie was it? And what did he use to open the bottle?

The provocative author recalls the "Belgrade Days" which were held in Ljubljana in July, 1980:

> *A fearsome noise in the square in front of the invisible monument and Robba's Fountain. Songs which I don't understand and wild screams, language that I don't understand. [...] Uncouth behaviour is attested by the screams, especially the thousands of coarse Serbian oaths, as if the world championships in sacrilegious swearing, vulgarity and defying Heaven were being held in front of the town hall. Wild drumming and deafening noise coming out of the amplifiers. Anti-music... This anti-music in front of the town hall contained no soft tones, as were once known by Gallus, Dolar, and Novak [the "Slovenian" classical music canon]. A thick blue cloud floats above the heads of the people and the sickening smell of tallow and Turkish čevaps is everywhere.*
>
> *In the faint which suddenly overwhelms me I see the camps of the sultans Bajazit and Murat on ancient European soil. [...]*
>
> *In these evening hours, fleeing with corpses on their shoulders, I ask myself whose idiotic idea was it to change our city into Bajazit and Murat's amusement park, in which everything which we have created in a century in Ljubljana will disappear, to give up with our creation our desire for beauty, peace, order, and spiritual development. In the name of the spirit of European civilization and culture. In my predicament I wonder what would happen if a Slovene were to start selling pork sausages or minced lard in the bazaars of Istanbul or Teheran? But what should I do with these jokes and visions of Turkish encampments!*[119]

---

119 Bojan Štih, "To ni nobena pesem, to je ena sam ljubezen" [That's Not a Poem, That's Just Love], *Naši razgledi*, June 11, 1982, 382. The same event was described in an article entitled "Do We Still Know How to Have Fun?" as follows: "Ljubljana for several days hosted a Belgrade *Skadarija* with everything that word means to Belgradians. The Ljubljanans went crazy with excitement, in front of the City Hall was the flavour of Serbian specialties and an atmosphere of Balkan unrestraint. European uptightness drowned in the sounds of old folk songs, and although the operating hours of the Skadarija bars 'Dva jelena' and 'Ima dana' soon sparked complaints from the neighbouring residents regarding the legal regulations, an infectious pride remained." (Igor Guzelj, "Se še znamo zabavati?" [Do We Still Know How to Have Fun?], *Teleks*, August 1, 1980, 27)

This text, as is borne witness to by a special folder containing responses to this article in the *Delo* archive, sparked off a huge controversy in almost all of the Yugoslav print media of the day, and even made it into some foreign papers. In the (pro-)Yugoslav newspaper *Borba* (Battle), an article appeared under the title "'The Enlightened' Štih" which read: "Or how writer and cultural worker Bojan Štih meditates in *Naši razgledi* about the filthy (pagan) effects of Serbian čevapčiči on Ljubljana's cultural heritage, in disunited Slovenia, about a nation which is dying out[.]"[120] In the Belgrade paper *Danas* (Today), an article appeared with the telling title "Ćevap with a Nationalist Flavour."[121]

What about the burek? Well, it doesn't appear either in Štih's text or in the numerous polemics. Ten years later such a controversy probably couldn't have happened without the burek. But let's stay in the eighties for a while. At the beginning?

When it arrived in Slovenia, the burek was an immigrant dish. This probably holds for both bureks (and pies) made in immigrant families (which occurs to nearly the same extent today) and for the bureks which were sold at the first burek stands. There had been burek stands in Slovenia since at least the first half of the 1960s.[122] As some interviewees

120 J. Pjević, "'Prosvijećeni' Štih" ['The Enlightened' Štih], *Borba*, July 6, 1992.

121 Meri Štajduhar, "Ćevap nacionalističkog okusa" [Ćevap with a Nationalist Flavour], *Danas*, August 10, 1982, 48.

122 In *Večer* we find one of the first mentions of bureks in an article entitled "First Encounter with the Burek." The article, published in 1958, which relates a Maribor native's first encounter with a Belgrade burek and the technical difficulties of eating it (the author first attacked it with a fork, leaving a greasy stain on his clothes), continues: "Since then I have eaten bureks only with my hands and nobody minds. Actually I am not currently eating bureks, since I am currently in Maribor and there are no bureks here." (Leteči, "Prvi spopad z burekom" [First Encounter with the Burek], *Večer*, December 13, 1958, 3) Which of course does not necessarily mean that nobody was then selling bureks in the Styrian capital, as we know they were there in the early sixties. In an article which criticizes the limited range of cheeses available in Slovenia, we read the following: "the burek, for instance, took nearly 40 years—from 1918 to just about 1960—to 'penetrate' the Maribor marketplace (Dežurni reporter [On-Call Reporter], "Sir" [Cheese], *Večer*, June 23, 1967, 2). Thus it was begun to be served at least as early as 1962 in the "Center self-service restaurant" (D. M., "Prve izkušnje samopostrežne restavracije v Mariboru" [First Impressions of a Self-Service Restaurant in Maribor], *Večer*, November 10, 1962, 4), at least as early as 1963 at the "snack bar at the Hotel Slavija" (M. M., "Poznajo gostinsko abecedo" [They Know Their Restaurant ABCs], *Večer*, October 23, 1963, 2), and the first burekrecipe also appears in *Večer* in 1963 (Anon., "Jutri na mizi" [On the Table Tomorrow], *Večer*, March 6, 1963, 4), in 1965 a "sales pavilion" opened in Maribor with bureks at the "Sabid private sweet shop" (B. P., "Vsak dan sveži burek v Mariboru" [Fresh Bureks Every Day in Maribor], *Večer*, May 29, 1965, 4), in 1966 the newspaper pub-

recalled, in the eighties the burek began to become popular among "non-immigrants," usually those whom according to Peter Stankovič had not become enthralled with the nationalist euphoria and the Yugophobia associated with it. These were mainly students, punks and urban youth in general. At the level of meanings this meant, as Stankovič continues, "that soon the burek no longer signified merely ethnic differences (between 'us' and 'them,' 'Slovenes' and 'non-Slovenes'), but also those Slovenes who did not have any major problems with the presence of immigrants from the other republics of former Yugoslavia."[123] But there is something we need to underscore here. According to conversations with numerous protagonists of the urban subcultures in the eighties, in those days the burek was not a symbolic object within various subculture groups and wasn't even a prominent, significant part of subcultural consumption. Gregor Tomc, who was part of the "generation of punks from the late 70s who had already become worn out in the 80s, with the help of the police," says that "among the punks," food was not a part of subcultural expression. "Drinking alcohol was part of the subculture, mainly in the form of beer, mainly at the Union coffee shop, at the railroad station, Medeks, FV, etc."[124] Ali Žerdin, of the generation "which was politically and culturally socialized at the time of the first Novi rok [New Rock] festival in 1981," has the following to say about the burek:

> *The thing with the burek is in my opinion more a coincidence than anything else. It was just that the only thing open at the train station at one in the morning was a kiosk which sold bureks and nothing else. So we sometimes went out for a burek. And when I say sometimes, I mean maybe once a year. I lived in Brod, so if I*

lished a photograph of the new Maribor burekproducer Nikola Djoni cutting a burek, who along with meat, cheese and apple bureks also promised to make bureks "stuffed with cherries, raisins, squash and boiled cabbage" (B. P., "Preizrenski Burek iz Slovenske ulice" [Prizren Bureks from a Slovenian Street], *Večer*, May 18, 1966, 4). In 1971, *Večer* published an ad in which the Gostinsko podjetje Ljubljana [Ljubljana Food Service Company] in point seven offered employment to a "burek-baker" under the following conditions: "skilled at making bureks, probationary period 2 months" (Anon., "Gostinsko podjetje Ljubljana, Ljubljana, Streliška ulica 12, vabi k sodelovanju" [Ljubljana Food Service Company, Ljubljana, Streliška Street 12, Invitation to Participate], *Večer*, November 19, 1971, 6).

123 Peter Stankovič, "Burek? Ja, bitte!" *Dnevnik, Zelena pika*, January 15, 2005, 36–37.

124 Gregor Tomc, e-mail message to author, 16 March, 2005.

> *wanted to go to the station, I had to go out of my way. But I usually didn't. If there was another kiosk selling something else at one in the morning, I might have gone for polenta.*[125]

And it was no different outside of Ljubljana. Boris Čibej remembers "the punk days in Idrija," a small, provincial Slovenian mining town: "At least as far as the group of people who I was hanging out with at the time went, there was no 'food-fetishism,' unless we count alcohol, which we were not too choosy about, as food. The only important category was price/performance."[126]

So we can assume that the great majority of people who ate bureks (or the great majority of those who didn't eat them) probably did not see it as an explicitly political act. For the urban youth of the eighties as well as all the rest who only occasionally went out for bureks, they represented calories and not symbols. Usually something warm for a belly full of alcohol, something cheap for shallow pockets. And something that was available even during the most impossible hours among the already scanty offerings of the 1980s. It should be emphasized that in those days, late at night and early in the morning, bureks (along with hot dogs, French fries, and not a whole lot else) were the only warm food available in most Slovenian cities.

The essential point of this story of calories without symbols is that the Balkan, southern burek had found its way onto Slovenian streets, and insinuated itself into the hands and mouths of the non-immigrant, indigenous, native population. And from here on, in my opinion, the story of the burek and the national essence starts to become increasingly interesting and complex; from here on is where the meta-burek can begin to fully develop and flourish.

Therefore the meanings that the burek predominantly defined throughout the nineties and probably those that most vocally accompany it today, were not the products of burek eaters. There was and still is a national or nationalist discourse at work, which couldn't and didn't want to take the burek as its own, as 'ours.' In other words, it was

125 Ali Žerdin, e-mail message to author, March 31, 2005.
126 Boris Čibej, e-mail message to author, April 2, 2005.

affronted by the presence, the conspicuousness of the burek on Slovenian streets, in the hands and mouths of youths and all the others who to a greater or lesser extent occasionally went out for a burek.

But it is perhaps an exaggeration, if not actually a mistake, to pin all of the blame for the parasitizing of the nationalist discourse on the burek, to hang the genesis of the ethno-nationally collared meta-burek on the appearance and presence of the burek on Slovenian streets. There could also have been other factors, although they are in my opinion much less significant ones, if they are significant at all. One example of this type of external factor is the silver medal won by Slovenian skier Jure Franko at the Olympics in Sarajevo in 1984—the first-ever medal for Yugoslavia at a winter Olympics. The aphorism "we love Jurek more than burek," which appeared at the time, and which is still remembered by many Slovenes and occasionally appears in comical, humorous contexts in Slovenian media,[127] popular culture and everyday speech, certainly brought the burek closer to Slovenes and perhaps also slightly stirred up Slovene-Yugoslav relations.

In this discussion of the genesis of nationalist discourse we also have to mention Slovenia's attaining of independence. This point, this date (June 25, 1991), signified the end of the official Yugoslav discourse about brotherhood and unity.[128] And of course we mustn't forget that nationalism, in the form of popular and other discourses, was present during the eighties, as well as before.[129] The meta-burek is not something that appeared upon Slovenia's attaining of independence. But

---

127 When Jure Franko visited Sarajevo again 22 years later, the (Slovenian) newspaper *Nedeljski Dnevnik* published an article entitled "We Love Jurek More than Burek!" (i.e. in Serbo-Croatian) (Toni Fornezzi, "Volimo Jureka više od bureka!" [We Love Jurek More than Burek!], *Nedeljski dnevnik*, February 26, 2006, 14). An article in the newspaper *Večer* about a round-table discussion entitled "Slovenes and the Balkans: on the Europeanization of Slovenian Society and Running Away from the Balkans" was titled "From Jure to Burek and Other Stories" (Matija Stepišnik, "Od Jureta do bureka in druge zgodbe" [From Jure to Burek and Other Stories], *Večer*, November 25, 2002, 5).

128 Igor Grdina, *Vladarji, lakaji, bohemi* [Rulers, Footmen, Boheminas] (Ljubljana: Studia Humanitatis, 2001), offers a critical treatment of the meaning of the slogan "Brotherhood and Unity."

129 For instance Gorazd Stariha in an article entitled "Dvigam to čašo za bratstvo in enotnost naših narodov" [I raise this Cup to the Brotherhood and Unity of our Nations], *Zgodovina za vse* 13, no. 2 (2006): 83–114, through an analysis of documents kept in the archives of the Petty Offenses Magistrate in Radovljica and the Radovljica District Court demonstrated that as early as the fifties in upper Gorenjska there were several cases of expressions of intolerance, chicanery, and other events going as far as physical violence directed at immigrants from other republics of the SFRY.

it was undoubtedly independence—of course together with all of the changes and social and cultural shocks—that was the historical event which, as I will show below, placed the meta-burek into a new, much more complex field and, in my opinion, also caused it to flourish.

Finally, let's take a bite into burekstatements. When exactly did the burek begin to invite meanings connected with someone or something ethnic or national? Meanings which it had always had—or at least from the moment it appeared in a foreign environment and was noticed there? In one of the first statements about the manufacturing of bureks by bakeries, which I found in a Slovenian newspaper from 1980, we also find this probably not mean-spirited formulation: "The people of Celje have received the 'domestic' burek very favourably[.]"[130] Therefore, if there is such a thing as a "domestic" burek, put in quotation marks not without reason, then there must also be such a thing as a "foreign" burek.

But from the mid-eighties onward the burek began with increasing currency to take on the role of a signifier of culture, cultures, the populations of the other republics of the former SFRY or the "Juga" [the South]. The less-worthy Juga population and culture? Let's leave that aside for now. In the song *Jasmina* by one of the most popular Slovenian pop groups from the eighties, Agropop, after the chorus with an emphasized Balkan melody, sung in Serbo-Croatian, which sings of love for Jasmina, a female voice—Jasmina—sings the following (in Slovene):

He was indeed a real man,
He reeked horribly of horse.
His back was really hairy,
He took me out for a cheese burek.[131]

In Miha Remec's cult science-fiction novel *Mana* [Manna], published in 1985, the painter Robi brings a burek to the novel's protagonist, journalist Jurij Jereb, who has a habit of complaining about, cursing and spitting on southerners. He accompanies it with the following words: "I have brought you some breakfast. A Balkan burek, so that you learn

130 -k, "Burek iz gaberske pekarne" [Bureks from the Gaberska Bakery], *Večer*, September 11, 1980, 6.
131 Aleš Klinar and Urban Centa, "Jasmina," *Agropop, Pesmi s Triglava* (ZKP RTV Slovenija, 1986).

right from the beginning where you belong. You can rinse it down with a Scotch whiskey, so that you can enjoy the feeling of still having one foot in Europe."[132] In both of these cases the burek therefore connotes something which is other, foreign to the Slovenian essence, but at the same time, something that—at least apparently—it has (already) inescapably accepted and which also determines it. It seems that our national essence exists in an indelible dependency on the Other, without which it cannot even establish itself. So what place in this otherness is given to the burek, how does it affect the national essence and what is permitted to be done with it?

Having left issues of political motivation aside to discuss these early statements, we can't avoid probably one of the most resonant early nationalist statements and one of the most resonant burekstatements in general, the graffito, "Burek? Nein danke." Before we deal with questions of the explicitness and implicitness and the motivations for nationalist statements, let's talk about this graffito for a moment. I would like to suggest, or in fact ask: is it possible that the super-symbolism of the burek, the complex meta-burek, is simply a coincidence? That is to say, if this graffito had never appeared, this graffito which due to its early appearance, its many years of being reproduced in various forms and environments, has very significantly and complexly consolidated and formed the burek's place in culture and thus its symbolic power, would the meta-burek be what it is today? This question of course also has various antecedents: Would such a burekstatement, of course not necessarily in the same form and syntagm, have appeared sooner or later, if some anonymous graffiti artist had not written it on a wall (for instance, if he had broken his arm or spent the money for the paint on booze), or to go even deeper into history, into the broader context, if the anti-nuclear slogan "Atom nein danke" had never appeared.[133] This question raises a further one: why did this happen to the burek? I could go on with these questions and to be honest I'm not sure where they would lead. However, I should

---

132 Miha Remec, *Mana. Časovni zapiski časnikarja Jurija Jereba* [Manna: Time Notes of Journalist Jurij Jereb] (Ljubljana: Tehniška založba Slovenije, 1985), 260.

133 The graffito "Burek? Nein danke" is most likely an adaptation of the famous European anti-nuclear slogan from the early eighties, "Atom nein danke."

Figure 5. "Burek? Nein danke." Photo by Aleš Erjavec. Courtesy of Aleš Erjavec.

reiterate the object of this question-posing section. The meta-burek—its genesis and ontology—is in my opinion partially a result of coincidences, which of course always occur within existing historical and material possibilities. To paraphrase Marx: people make their own meta-burek, but not just as they please, and not under conditions they choose by themselves. This is in no way a final, clear answer to my original question, which in my opinion does not allow any final, absolute answers.

So now we can finally address the apparent explicitness of this nationalist statement, which first appeared on a Ljubljana street in the second half of the eighties and has appeared occasionally on the walls of Ljubljana ever since. But is it really as explicit and direct as it seems at first glance? What if this graffito had originally been encoded, written on the wall of a building on Gosposka street, one of Ljubljana's most heavily traffic-laden streets, without any sort of nationalist pretense, as a more or less innocent joke, a gag, which was intended merely to poke fun at or even laugh at the developing nationalism. However, my guess is that the numerous reproductions of this graffito, which appeared on the walls of Ljubljana throughout the nineties, were mainly encoded and written by nationalist hands.

To begin with, I would like to express my scepticism or even disagreement with the idea that it is possible to simply and deterministically apply great truths and clear concepts, such as nationalism in this case, to anything as complex as culture. However, sometimes such application seems completely unproblematic, even mechanical. It could be described as a perfect noiseless translation, a literal translation in which not only is nothing lost, but nothing is added. A good example of such a malleable application, which at the same time has a highly motivated and clear political strategy, is revealed by the name of the project "Anti Burek System (ABS)" by the skinhead group SLOI, which, according to Marta Gregorič, sang their words in verse in pubs. That is, this group from the beginning of the nineties played without instruments.[134] "Anti Burek System" is clearly a very explicit, highly motivated, malleable burekstatement.[135]

Of course, such translations and applications—if we can even speak of one-way translations, applications of great truths, or of being self-evident—are most often unclear, ambiguous, and questionable.

---

134 Marta Gregorčič, "Vikingi ali Valhala—skinheadi Slovenije" [Vikings or Valhalla—Skinheads of Slovenia], in *Urbana plemena. Subkulture v Sloveniji v devetdesetih* [Urban Tribes: Subcultures in Slovenia in the Nineties], ed. Peter Stankovič, Gregor Tomc, and Mitja Velikonja (Ljubljana: Študentska založba, 1999), 104.

135 Skinheads and bureks!? Let's take a quick look at our neighbours. In a paper which discusses the intolerance of Croatian skinheads and the publication of the first issue of the "fanzine for skinhead culture" SH–ZG, we read: "In their magazine, the Zagreb skinheads published a contest with shocking content. The participants in the contest would compete by collecting the names of gay clubs, Chinese restaurants, Orthodox municipalities, sweetshops, and burek stands. When all the names had been collected, they would publish a skinhead multicultural guide to Zagreb. According to the publishers of the contest, the guide was intended for both tourists and skinheads, so that they could 'take care of things' quarter by quarter." (Peter Žerjavič, "Lov na tujce in geje" [Hunting for Foreigners and Gays], *Delo*, December 31, 2003, 24.)

However, within this, the burek—here more in a nationalist than in an ethno-national context—can signify a lot of things, as has already been demonstrated in countless examples. It can be filled with very different content. It is a kind of hollow dough into which fillings can to some extent or within certain conditions be added at will. What sort of fillings?

Bosnians, Bosniaks—here I mean the ethnic affiliation or identity—as we can read in the story "How a Bosnian Loves," which tells of three Bosnians in Slovenia and their three blow-up sex dolls:

> *Soon Fikret and Mirza also came from their birthplace. They rented a flat together and created an island of nostalgia, a true Little Bosnia, in the middle of their urban neighbourhood. After some hard work it was just right. It smelled of freshly ground coffee, cigarette smoke swirled beneath the ceiling, there was fresh burek on the tray, and the Bosnian national anthem emanated from the speakers. The heroes' hearts warmed and they perked up their ears. The neighbours,' of course.*[136]

Albanians, derogatorily called "Šiptarji" [Shiptars], as depicted in an image from the weekly magazine *Mladina* [Youth], and published in the humour column Manipulator, which features jokes with exclusively Serbo-Albanian motifs, or, as the following amusing tale tells us:

> *Schollmayer [a well-known Slovenian businessman] was also known to be exceptionally rude. In an interview with the sports magazine Ekipa he said: "Some 'Shiptar' bought that company (SGP Galjevica), and doesn't do anything, all he does is sue us for the principal, which was 2.5 million tolars, now it's 30 million." Dragan Lazić, the Commercial Manager of SGP Galjevica, recognized himself in the description of a Shiptar who doesn't do anything. He told journalists: "My business acquaintances have started to ask me when I'm going to bring them bureks."*[137]

136 nm, "Kako ljubi Bosanec" [How a Bosnian Loves], *Hopla*, November 21, 2003, 55.
137 Nejc Praprotnik, "Jurij Schollmayer," 32.

Figure 6. An Albanian. Anon., in "Manipulator," *Mladina*, December 15, 1989, 12. Courtesy of *Mladina*.

Muslim immigrants, as we can see in this photoshopped image (Figure 7) of dark-skinned men in Ljubljana, published in a humour column in *Mladina* called "Mladinamit". The headline reads: "Will trade bureks for a mosque!" and the words on the sign in broken Slovenian/English: "No mosque for us, no burek for you."[138]

The Balkans, as we can read in letters to the editor in the most popular Slovenian newspaper *Delo*: "Then he took the role of a paper tiger, although he could easily have prevented the last Balkan war. Perhaps it would actually have happened if the Balkans were known for their oil and not for bureks and kajmak!"[139]

---

138 Anon., photo montage, in Berto Ritotreb, "Mladinamit," *Mladina*, January 12, 2004, 72.

139 Aleksander Nardin, "Zgodovina se ponavlja" [History is Repeating Itself], *Delo*, May 6, 2004, 5.

Figure 7. "Will trade bureks for a mosque!" Anon., in Berto Ritotreb, "Mladinamit," *Mladina*, January 12, 2004, 72. Courtesy of *Mladina*.

The continuity of the former Yugoslav political system, as we can read in the humour supplement to *Večer* entitled "Toti List":

> *Whoever doesn't read shouldn't eat, said the leader for life of our republic Milan Kučan in an interview for the Saturday supplement to Toti list, when speaking of his cooking skills. "Čevapčiči with onions, burek & barbecue, are more important for communists than the battle for Šentilj [one of the most significant operations in the ten-day "war of independence" in Slovenia]. A truly mild taste, not recommended for the battle against the white vermin," added court "poet" Ciril Zlobec[.]*[140]

The Orient, as we can read in the *Dictionary of Slovenian Literary Language*, "Oriental cake made of pastry dough with filling: burek with cheese; burek with meat."[141]

Etc.

---

140 Anon., *Večer*, July 29, 1998, 42.

141 Anon., "Burek," in *Slovar slovenskega knjižnega jezika. Prva knjiga* [Dictionary of Slovenian Literary Language: First Volume], ed. Anton Bajec et. al. (Ljubljana, DZS, 1970), 226.

Of course in such an analysis of the meta-burek we have to continually ask, for each case separately, what strategies, if any, the individual statements support. For all of the above statements it would be hard to say that they are clearly, explicitly politically or nationalistically motivated. But for all of them it seems that some kind of implicit strategy of domination is at work. A strategy of naturalization, the essentialization of differences and identities. A strategy of symbolic violence, or in short, stereotyping.

In order for an identity to exist there must be a distinction between it and another, and here it seems that it is not even very important what we fill it with. It could be simply a difference in the way one eats, either with or without added sugar, as the Bosnian immigrant Božo, the hero of the film *Kajmak in marmelada* [Cheese and Jam], learns in a comical manner. *Kajmak in marmelada*, one of the most popular "Slovenian" films of all time, tells of the (in)compatibility of the partnership between Slovene Špela and immigrant Božo. What do you think Božo calls the things the mother of "his" Slovenian Špela cooks, which all Slovenes cook? "Burek sa šećerom" ("burek with sugar" in Serbo-Croatian)—a strudel (i.e. a pastry which is the product of German cuisine, and an important part of Slovenian cuisine).[142]

Of course I am not saying here that differences in the ways of eating, cooking, and other material and non-material practices between ethnic, national, and other groups do not exist. What I am trying to say is that the invention of meanings is not arbitrary; it doesn't occur in a vacuum, it is not without reference, as is naïvely assumed by (too) numerous constructivism-oriented social scientists. But the fact that meanings cannot be invented at will does not mean that the burek has some kind of essential, absolute meaning.

Here it would perhaps not be amiss to ask once again why the burek is so often reached for when fleshing out these differences. Is it just its widespread popularity, its conspicuousness? Or is there some more sophisticated, perverse strategy at work here? A strategy which

142 Branko Djurić, *Kajmak in marmelada* [Cheese and Jam] (ATA Productions, 2003).

through fixing meaning at the level of nutrition naturalizes the essence of immigrants at the level of primary needs, i.e. biology?[143]

Let's return for a moment to the film, which is (excessively) richly structured on stereotypes, as film critic Marcel Štefančič tells us in his colourful review:

> *The Bosnian (Branko Đurić) in Cheese and Jam finds a Slovenian girl (Tanja Ribič) mainly for romantic reasons. Then he loses her. And then gets her back again. Clearly, in between we will get a lecture on comparative ethnology. Before you can say "Na planincah" [In the Hills, a traditional Slovenian song], they are already telling endless jokes about Mujo [a stereotypical Bosnian figure in Yugoslav humour] & a Slovene: Bosnians are lazy, they steal, they don't clean up after themselves, they drink in public, pick their noses and eat bureks—while Slovenians work two jobs, insist on eating beef soup, sing national folk songs, blow German tourists, commit suicide, and eat bureks with sugar (i.e. strudel). Wow, good thing they're both atheists.*[144]

But, you'll say, the writer and director of this film is a Bosnian immigrant to Slovenia. Pretty complicated, ain't it? Well, maybe not. Through induction we can conclude that stereotypes (also) affect the self-recognition of those who are the subjects of stereotyping. This however means that stereotypes (can) have real consequences.[145] Of

143 This question was impressed upon me by Frantz Fanon, "The Negro and Psychopathology," in *Identity: A Reader*, ed. Paul du Gay, Jessica Evans, and Peter Redman (London: Open University, Sage, 2000). In his study of (stereotypical) representations of black people he points out that the concentration of meaning around their genitalia fixes the essence of blacks at the physical level, in contrast with representations of whites, which are usually focused on intellect.

144 Marcel Štefančič, Jr., "Kajmak in marmelada" [Cheese and Jam], *Mladina*, November 17, 2003, 74.

145 Regarding the issue of the consequences of stereotypical representations, we should mention a study by Ayse Caglar, "McDoner: Doner Kebap and the Social Positioning Struggle of German Turks," in *Marketing in a Multicultural World: Ethnicity, Nationalism, and Cultural Identity*, ed. Janeen Arnold Costa and Gary J. Bamossy (Thousand Oaks: Sage, 1995), which is particularly close to the subject of this chapter. The paper shows how the "doner kebab," which was brought to Germany by Turkish immigrants, played a central role in the recognition of the migrant group. At the places where Turks first sold doner kebabs as an exotic ethnic food (which was mainly bought by Germans) and was used as a positive symbol of cultural connection in multicultural discourse, the effects of the changing attitude towards foreigners led to a loosening of the association between "Turkishness" and the doner kebab. Stands and chains appeared with names

course, such induction can be highly problematic. We could conclude all kinds of things from the above example, for instance that Bosnians make rude jokes at the expense of Slovenes, and therefore have to be silenced. However, numerous statements tell us that the burek has become an important element in the self-recognition of immigrants, Bosnians, Albanians, and all the rest. In a profile of the Albanian academically trained painter Gani Llallos, who lives in Ljubljana, we read: "Only through an ironic question do we arrive at the most common Slovenian stereotype about Albanians: 'What would Slovenians be without bureks and baklava?'"[146] Again, as Karl Marx would say: "They cannot represent themselves, they must be represented."[147]

Of course, even those who usually represent others cannot always represent. Here I do not mean (only) that stereotyping is not just a tool of the power of the more dominant in the process of signification,[148] but above all that the superiors in some power relations can be subordinate in others. In an interview about negative images in the promotion of Slovenian tourism, Slovene ethnologist Dr. Janez Bogataj responded:

> *Let's take the stereotypical presentation of Slovenian cuisine. The London newspaper* The Guardian *reported that our culinary specialties are burek and brandy. I ask myself where the British obtained this information and what Slovenia will do now. Will the disinformation which was published be rescinded and the truth about our cuisine published free of charge? Did the STO [Slovenian Tourism Organization] invite the journalist from* The Guardian *to*

like McKebap and Donerburger. At the same time, "doner" became a sobriquet for Turks. A multicultural youth festival in Berlin in 1987 was called "Disco doner," and the following slogan appeared in controversies about foreigners (Ausländerfrage): "Kein doner ohne Ausländer!" [No kebabs without foreigners!]. Amidst this political chaos the doner kebab sold better than ever. But for Turks the continued association with it means a further denial of their increasing social mobility. The final irony is that in their attempts to loosen and move away from the association with the doner kebab, the sellers of this food have moved into selling Italian food.

146 Tea Černe, "Le kaj bi Slovenci brez bureka in baklave?" [What Would Slovenians Be without Bureks and Baklava?], *Nedelo*, November 9, 2003, 24.

147 Marx, *The Eighteenth Brumaire*, 106.

148 In this context I should add that stereotyping generally occurs in places where there is a clear inequality, that is, major differences in the power of groups (cf., for example Stuart Hall, "The Spectacle of the 'Other,'" in *Representation: Cultural Representations and Signifying Practises*, ed. Stuart Hall [London: Sage, 2002], 258).

> *Slovenia or at least send him professional materials and tell him where we Slovenians are on the map of European professional cuisine?*[149]

It was therefore no surprise that the burek and brandy appeared in the subheading to this long interview—an interview which offers a great deal of other material for subheadings: "The task of Slovenian tourism policy has to be to find new ways to implement visible projects which arise as early as the study phase—the British are spreading the delusion that the jewels of Slovenian cuisine are bureks and brandy."

Stereotypical representation is therefore undoubtedly a place where power intrudes into processes of signification. And more than it would appear! According to Stuart Hall, the social and symbolic orders are maintained through stereotyping.[150] But instead of repeating, proclaiming and name-dropping these lofty, authoritative ideas, it seems to me to be more useful to return to the issue at hand, that is, the burek and the meta-burek.

At this point it would be fruitful to invite Edward Said to join the debate. With his inestimable assistance it would be possible to establish a kind of "burekalism," i.e., "a style of thought based on an ontological and epistemological distinction made between"[151] a population and place defined by the burek and a population and place not defined by the burek. In order not to lose our place in these long sentences, our last paring of definitions will be translated, contracted to the conceptually not completely equivalent categories adapted to the needs of this research: "immigrants" and "Slovenes." To continue with Said's thoughts and words, the concept of burekalism as I conceive it deals principally not with a correspondence between burekalism and the burek, but with the internal consistency of burekalism and its ideas about the burek, despite or beyond any correspondence, or lack thereof, with a "real" burek.[152] And furthermore, to believe that the burek was created

---

149 Manfred Meršnik, "Zgrešeno mnenje, da nimamo kadrov" [The Erroneous Opinion that We Lack the Human Resources], *Večer*, September 15, 2004, 33.

150 Hall, "The Spectacle of the 'Other,'" 258.

151 Said, *Orientalism*, 2.

152 Ibid, 5.

or burekalized simply as a necessity of the imagination is, I believe, mistaken, or as Said said, "disingenuous."[153] The relationship between the burek and the non-burek "is a relationship of power, of domination, of varying degrees of a complex hegemony,"[154] which is nicely indicated by the title of this chapter: "The Dictatorship of the Carniolan Sausage." The burek was burekalized not just because it was established that it is "foreign," "Balkan," in short "bureky," but also because it was possible—that is, that it was forced to the point where it was possible—to make it foreign, Balkan, bureky. The people defined by the burek, that is, immigrants, very rarely speak (about the burek) on their own behalf. And when they do speak, it seems that they usually speak in a way that is suitable for non-burek defined people, i.e., Slovenes. Think back to *Kajmak in marmelada* and the profile of the academically trained Albanian painter. Of course, what most frequently obtains is Marx's famous motto, quoted above: that non-burek defined people speak on behalf of burek defined people and also represent them. Just look at the list presented above. It is truly fascinating that in all of these countless colourful burekstatements in the media, statements which put the burek into the family or wider milieu of immigrant communities in Slovenia almost never appear.[155] Immigrants never or almost never make burekstatements in the media, except in statements which reproduce burekalism (for instance, the jokes by Branko Djurić in the film *Kajmak in marmelada*), i.e., statements which are custom-made for Slovenes. On the other hand there is a huge pile of different types of stories in which bureks are "discovered" in foreign countries, and which expose well-known Slovenian individuals and families making and eating bureks. (However, it seems that there is perhaps a more insidious strategy at work here. But more on that later.)

---

153 Ibid.

154 Ibid.

155 The only such example that I found is a report on the celebration of Ramadan in Jesenice, which deals to a great extent with fasting and eating during this period of fasting, as indicated by the title of the article ("Fasting and Abundance during Ramadan"). The description of *iftar*—the supper which follows an all-day fast—(of course) included cheese and meat bureks (see Urška Mlinarič, "Post in obilo dobrot ob ramadanu" [Fasting and Abundance during Ramadan], *Večer*, November 29, 2002, 14.).

This brings us to the next limitation, and I should remind the reader that I am still leaning heavily on Said's *Orientalism*. One ought never to assume that the structure of burekalism is nothing more than a structure of lies or myths which, were the truth about them to be told, would simply evaporate. We must try to grasp the sheer combined power of burekalized discourse, and its fearsome and awe-inspiring durability. Burekalism is much more than a collection of falsifications and lies, it is not just an airy Slovenian fantasy about the burek, but a corpus of theory and practice in which a considerable amount of material investment has been made. This continuous investment has made burekalism, as a system of self-evidence, knowledge, and signification, into an accepted structure through which the burek is filtered into Slovenian consciousness. And that same investment has multiplied the number of statements proliferating out from burekalism into the culture in general.[156]

Burekalism, still following Said, therefore depends for its strategy on a flexible positional superiority, which puts the non-burek defined person (Slovene) into a whole series of possible relationships with the burek without his ever losing the relative upper hand.[157] Starting in the second half of the eighties within the umbrella of the domination, hegemony, and superiority of non-burek defined people over burek-defined people there emerged a complex burek, i.e. a meta-burek, essentially suitable for the entertainment and metaphorical needs of popular culture, the media, colloquial language, publicists, literature, and so on. To return again to Said, burekalism is therefore not a mere political subject matter or a field which is reflected passively by culture, language, or place; nor is it a large and diffuse collection of texts about the burek; nor is it representative and expressive of some nefarious Slovenian plot to hold down immigrants, Southerners, and Balkan people. It is rather a distribution of superiority, dominance, geopolitical and politico-cultural awareness into popular culture, colloquial and other language, entertainment, the media, literature, art, and elsewhere.[158]

156 Said, *Orientalism*, 5.
157 Ibid, 7.
158 Ibid, 12.

And yet, one must repeatedly ask oneself whether what matters in burekalism, still following Said, is the general group of ideas overriding the mass of material—about which who could deny that they were shot through with doctrines of Slovenian superiority, various kinds of racism, nationalism, etc., dogmatic views of "the burek" as a kind of ideal and unchanging abstraction?—or the much more varied work produced by almost uncountable individual writers, whom one would take up as individual instances of authors dealing with, touching on and tripping over the burek.[159]

I think that in the case of burekalism both are true. It is conditioned by both a dogmatic group of ideas and by the creativity and originality of individual authors. But I also think that between dogmatism and productivity, at least on a certain manifest level, there is an important difference, which is also reflected in methodological limitations: that is, they cannot be dealt with using the same tools. Burekalism thus pretends to be something relaxed, productive, and open, and on the other hand, it secretively conceals its strict, closed, orthodox nature. It pretends to be a trifle, but the limitations which are invisibly created indicate its power. A power which should not be underestimated. First of all, this limiting is related to the fact that burekalism dictates, as we have already mentioned, which things should be noticed and emphasized, and which should be silenced and unobserved. This analysis of silence is, however, a problematic, tricky, never completely convincing and consistent task. It is e.g. difficult to say how much substance burekalism contributed to a particular silence, if anything at all. For instance, nowhere, either in the media or in everyday speech or in professional and scientific literature, have I found any mention or even hint of there being a dish or several different dishes whose form or style of preparation was very similar to a burek, even under a different name or names, in the territory of present-day Slovenia before the arrival of immigrants during the time of the SFRY.[160] But it does not appear to be the case that all foods keep so

159 Ibid, 8.

160 Various sorts of pies made from pastry dough which are similar to bureks in appearance, preparation, and ingredients were popular primarily in the south-western and south-eastern parts of Slovenia (for example, *prleška oljovica, presni kolač, pršjača, belokranjska povitica, prosta povitica*). These are mainly holiday ritual foods and foods prepared at the end of major farming tasks.

silent about their similarities, connections or relatedness to other foods. For instance, when I asked in pubs in Prekmurje about "retaš" (a pie well known in the Prekmurje region), I often received the categorical response that it is a strudel. A strudel, which was developed in southern German and Austrian cuisine! These two examples of course suggest a number of other, primarily developmental-historical, contextual questions, which demand specific and precise treatment, and for which therefore there is no time or space here. However, we can pose one question. Did burekalism have anything to do with this avoidance of Slovenian dishes having similarities to the burek in the Slovenian ethnic territory?

Furthermore, burekalism dictates, and, it seems, dictates very specifically, where the burek belongs and where it does not, what kinds of opportunities bureks are appropriate for and what kinds they are not, and in what ways. So where does it not belong?

Clearly it does not belong in the *Slovenski etnološki leksikon* [Slovenian Ethnological Dictionary], in which we find slang words such as *avtostop* (hitchhiking), *avtostopar* (hitchhiker), *disco klub, golf, grafit* (graffiti), *hitra hrana* (fast food), *lepotni ideal* (the ideal of beauty), *letoviščar* (holidaymaker), *nakupovalni center* (shopping centre), *nudistični kamp* (nudist camp), *papiga* (parrot), *pedikura* (pedicure), *piknik, Ponterosso, rally, sex shop, sindikalni izlet* (trade union excursion), and many other pop-culture phenomena. And there are dishes such as *grahornjak, krapec, kuc-kruh, kvasenica, kvocnjak, mauželj, mešta,* and *modnica,* which many Slovenes have never heard of. Well, that should be enough to flummox you. You can find them all in the *Leksikon,* next to perennial Slovenian favourites *potica* cakes and Carniolan sausage, but, as noted above, not next to the burek.[161]

It would also seem that the burek does not belong in Slovenian cookbooks. But we have to be careful here. We have mentioned the relatively

---

Of course, technical and other similarities cannot be an argument for this or any other kind of influence or even for a shared origin of the foods. Filled pies made of pastry dough—including the burek—can also be found in other Slavic nations, while cakes made of short pastry dough or leavened dough are characteristic of other, primarily central European nations (Janez Bogataj, e-mail messages to author, April 11 and 12, 2007). Of course, a burek is not necessarily a filled pie, as there are also spiral rolled bureks.

161 Angelos Baš, ed., *Slovenski etnološki leksikon* [Slovenian Ethnological Dictionary] (Ljubljana: Mladinska knjiga, 2004).

large number of burekrecipes on the Internet and in magazines. However, burekdenial slaps you in the face in both cookbooks that contain the root "Sloven-" in their titles, and more general cookbooks written for or adapted to Slovene cooks. The place of the burek in Slovenian nutritional ideology is therefore (still) exceedingly, to put it mildly, marginal. And thus it still waits behind the closed doors which lead to the more hallowed world of cookbooks—i.e., sacred (Slovenian) books and not just the plebeian world of magazines and the Internet. In a survey of several dozen cookbooks I found a recipe for burek only in *Kuhinja naše družine* [Our Family Cuisine].[162] Perhaps it would not be out of place to mention here that the majority of these cookbooks, which are in one way or another adapted to Slovene cooks, also do not contain any recipes for immigrant dishes, i.e. dishes from the republics of the former SFRY, which could not exactly be said of dishes from the West.

The burek also does not belong in numerous other national nutritional canons. For instance, we could not find it, as was established by newspaper reporter Ervin Hladnik-Milharčič, at the grandiose feast upon Slovenia's adopting of the euro, that is, a sort of gourmet welcome to the euro, which was prepared by 25 cooks, served by 60 waiters, and attended by 1350 guests, including ten European prime ministers, and at which 80 different dishes were served, including ham in dough which contained the banquet's basic message: the euro symbol. The journalist in question thus commented on the central object, the main course, which was given its own special table, "together with cooks, who with their long knives sliced always equal slices":

> *The culinary overview of European integrationist culture set at its core a piece of meat, which places Turkey outside the circle of enjoyment. Jewish culture also has nothing to find here. They could console themselves with lamb curry and ratatouille, but when going to get them they would have to give a wide berth to the table*

162 Stanko Grafenauer, *Kuhinja naše družine* [Our Family Cuisine] (Ljubljana: Mladinska knjiga, 2002), 195–196. Burekrecipes could probably be found more easily in various topical cookbooks; for instance we found one in Radojko Mrlješ et al., *Kuhinje Balkana: Razkošje okusov za vse priložnosti* [Cuisines of the Balkans: Luxury of Tastes for all Occasions] (Tržič: Učila International, 2005).

> *laden with prosciutto, and make sure they didn't accidentally brush up against the pork ribs, blood sausage, sausages, and everything that smells of a delicatessen. If you take the euro as the parameter of European understanding of its own foundations and everything that can be wrapped around it, then the advocates of the principle of exclusivity in the framing of the European constitution could be right. At the core of the European identity is a pig, which is undoubtedly a Christian animal. Despite its frequent appearance in popular culture, the burek did not find its way onto the menu in any of its popular forms.*[163]

Perhaps even more significant is the burek's role in places where we wouldn't expect it, i.e. in places where according to the criteria of nationalist discourse it does not belong.

In the Dictionary of Slovenian Literary Language, from an edition which otherwise requires special treatment, it is described as an "Oriental cake made of pastry dough with filling: burek with cheese; burek with meat."[164] An Oriental cake? The adjective should best be left alone, lest it raise too many unanswered questions. I will deal only with the noun, which reduces the burek from a main course in the main meal of the day—at least traditionally in the Balkans, in Turkey, and at least in some Arabic countries, where the dish is usually known under other names—to the level of a secondary dish, i.e. a cake.

The burek also appears in the Slovenian National Theatre, Drama Ljubljana—Slovenia's principal theatre, which is not at all surprising. What is more surprising is the play in which it appears. In *Smoletov vrt* [Smole's Orchard, a Slovenicized version of Chekov's *The Cherry Orchard*], which—as it says in the first line of the playbill—is "utterly saturated with 'Sloveneness,'"[165] the character Nebojša appears as a sort of

163 Ervin Hladnik-Milharčič, "Šunka v evru, 25 kuharjev, 60 natakarjev, 80 jedi in 1350 gostov" [Ham Shaped like a Euro, 25 Cooks, 60 Waiters, 80 Dishes and 1350 Guests], *Dnevnik, Objektiv*, January 20, 2007, 18.

164 Anon., "Burek," in *Slovar slovenskega knjižnega jezika. Prva knjiga* [Dictionary of Slovenian Literary Language: First Volume], ed. Anton Bajec et al. (Ljubljana: DZS, 1970), 226.

165 Jera Ivanc, "Slovenija, odkod lepote tvoje ..." [Slovenia, From Whence Comes Your Beauty ...], in *Smoletov vrt: komedija v treh dejanjih* [Smole's Orchard: Three Acts Comedy], ed. Meta Hočevar (Ljubljana: SNG Ljubljana, 2006), 7.

inventory of immigrant characteristics and behaviour. Sitting at a table laid for a holiday banquet, he explains how he went into a building with a sign over the door that said "Mestna hranilnica" [City Savings Bank] in order to "nahrani z mesom" [stuff himself with meat—the pun is based on the polysemy of the verb *hraniti*, which means both "to save" and "to feed"]:

> *Inside, all of the waiters were behind windows, like in some kind of bank. I asked one of them where I could get an "odrezak" [Serbo-Croatian for cut of meat]. 'Oh, "odrezek" [Slovenian for coupon or cut of meat],' he said. 'Yeah, a pork chop,' I replied. He looked at me a bit funny and said: 'First you have to fill out a form, take it to the window with your money, and there you will get a coupon.' Ever since then I have known that an "odrezek" is not a "zrezek" [i.e. cut of meat]. ... Then as usual I went to the train station for a burek and a real Turkish coffee.*[166]

From these brief analyses of non-statements, from weighing the burek's silence, we move to extremely loud statements. From places where the burek's presence is unexpected to places where its presence is fully expected.

Extreme nationalist representations can be found on that most plural of media, as the Internet is often called, more specifically in various online chat forums. But here too we quickly realize that the burek appears in its classical role as a signifier of southerners, "čefurji," Bosnians, in short, for a sort of inferior beings or their culture. The following emotional outburst was responded to concisely by an author who used the pseudonym "NIET, the BIG Kahuna," in one of the forums on the "Sloport" website, in a debate titled "ČEFURJI": "at least someone agrees with me... but I still like bureks anyhow."[167]

166 Meta Hočevar, "Smoletov vrt" [Smole's Orchard], in *Smoletov vrt: komedija v treh dejanjih* [Smole's Orchard: Three Acts Comedy], ed. Meta Hočevar (Ljubljana: SNG Ljubljana, 2006), 57.

167 Niet, accessed September 15, 2006, http://www.sloport.net/forum/viewthread.php?tid=5920&page=5#neprebrano.

Čefurčine should all be killed
they all impose their habits [on us]
their spitting and cursing
and another thing their craze for bureks when they hear it they start to sniff like dogs..and that's what they are!!!
and those shiptars [Albanians] who are all violent
they always want to beat somebody up ...and they're useless even
shit can be used as manure on a field

they should all be exterminated
italy even boasts about their growing popu...because of immigrantsw..pfff come on
if it goes on like this SLO will soon be called
Slovenska and Herzegovina
not to mention mosques oh yeah
we should build one
round them up from all over SLo

and then douse their heads with napalm until they meltt 

poor us in 10 years you go into a restaurant it'll be like mcdonalds in america burek burek big burek bureks horseburek cheeseburek salatsburekk and so on
WE'VE GOTTA DO SOMETHING ABOUT THEM THERE ISNT ANYONE WHO
HASNT HAD BAD EXPERIENCES WITH THEM
I SEE THEM WHEN THEY GO THROUGH THE JUNKYARDS TO COLLECT
THINGS AND NEXT TO THEM THE KIDS ARE PULLING ON CABLES

YEAH WELL THEYRE GOOD FOR ONE THING THEY ONLY KNOW HOW TO
BUILD
and one day ALL THE HOUSES will be MADE BY BOSNA

Of course, numerous nationalist statements are less explicit; they are not necessarily the direct product of the process of stereotyping and are not connected with the print, electronic, or other media. They can also refer more directly to the unconditioned burek. When bureks were served at Cankarjev dom (Slovenia's main cultural and congress centre) in 2003, at an exhibition marking the centennial of Slovenian graphic artist and painter Nikolaj Pirnat—of course much smaller, and thus more chic and fancy than those served at Slovenian burek stands and shops—a lot of comments as to their appropriateness were made among the general public.[168] So we can add one more place where bureks don't belong: the house of Slovenian culture, Cankarjev dom.

There is something I would like to add about this last example. This text probably gives the impression that the meta-burek is mainly the product of the media machine, as this fearsome complex is often called. But such an impression would be mistaken. It is spread by an eclectic, non-exclusive, for many an excessive type of analysis, which simply uses or consumes whatever comes to hand. And what comes to hand most easily are the media, especially the print media and the Internet, which hold a major lead over all the rest. Of course other fields, segments, and complexes are involved in the production of the meta-burek, in the genesis of burekstatements, which of course in very different

168 Ksenija Berk, telephone conversation, February 23, 2005.

ways generate the existence of statements in the field of memory, in the materiality of books, and in other forms of registration.

On the other hand, at least in the case of burekstatements we can detect a certain voracity, greediness, colonialism of the media. That is, numerous burekstatements which appeared independently of the media were sooner or later sucked into the media machine, and in one way or another transformed and recycled as media statements (for instance, "We love Jurek more than burek"). Furthermore, below we will see that many statements were just waiting for someone to bring them to the surface—therefore a class of potential statements, which were prepared and framed by other, non-media practices, fields, and complexes—which the media simply articulated and made visible. Out of these pre-statements, these potential statements, they made statements and undoubtedly enriched them, and to a great extent also took control of the analysis of those statements.

Let us therefore look at this nationalist statement-making from other, topical, thematic perspectives. And in doing so, let us pay attention to the Cyclopean power of the media—their ability to bring statements to the surface, to articulate statements from the community of ideas, worldviews, and thoughts.

The burek with its stands and its customers on the street is directly articulated in space, in architecture. The street kiosks, especially in the old town centre of Ljubljana, seem not to be just an aesthetic problem, but, with the meanings which these foreign things bear, are also an additional problem for the municipal, cultural, conservationist, artistic and media authorities. A well-known Slovenian commentator writes in the main Slovenian newspaper *Delo*:

> *The architectural and cultural heritage of the city thus falls into the hands of newcomers, "foreigners," who usually have no emotional relationship with it. [...] The structure of the population in the last few decades has thus changed ("worsened"?) so that there is simply no human soil in which to cultivate any central European values and lifestyles. [...] However: identity is an inner need of human beings, their internal home, so why shouldn't*

a city feel the same way? How do you convince an Albanian who sells bureks that Ljubljana has to return to its own identity?[169]

This unusually large photograph of a burek kiosk set up beneath the arcade at the Ljubljana marketplace—one of the treasured works of Slovenia's revered architect Jože Plečnik—also seems to be a challenge, as it covers nearly the entire upper half of the Culture section of *Delo*:[170]

Figure 8. Photo of a burek kiosk beneath the arcade at the Ljubljana marketplace. Blaž Samec, *Delo*, July 12, 2005, 9. Courtesy of *Delo*.

The photo is accompanied by the caption: "Plečnik's burek—This burek kiosk which is set up against regulations at the Ljubljana marketplace, which is a protected monument, is still standing despite the efforts of inspectors."[171] On the connotative level the photograph could be read as the creation of the perception that the burekkiosk with its enormous, threatening appearance is endangering Plečnik's sensuous and filigreed architecture (in fact the arcade is incomparably larger than

169 Boris Jež, "Razglednica iz Ljubljane" [Postcard from Ljubljana]. *Delo, Sobotna priloga*, September 18, 1999, 44.

170 Blaž Samec, photo, *Delo*, July 12, 2005, 9.

171 Anon., caption to Blaž Samec's photo, *Delo*, July 12, 2005, 9.

the kiosk). It is therefore a sort of cancerous architectural growth which would be best cut away from the hallowed architectural, national, central European, and numerous other landscapes.

We can also read about the unsuitable appearance of this kiosk in an article with the telling title "They Don't Give a Damn about Plečnik"[172] and elsewhere. The stumbling block is (was) not just the burekstand. In order not to go on for too long I shall give only a short excerpt from an article in *Delo*: "Nobel Burek [a burekstand in downtown Ljubljana] truly impoverishes the city centre, but because of its appearance and not its content."[173] The same stand appeared in the same newspaper, again in the Culture section, in a comic strip:[174]

Figure 9. The burekstand in a comic strip. Boris Jukič, *Delo*, July 18, 2005, 8. Courtesy of *Delo*.

The text reads:
Inspector: "Unprofessional construction work is destroying the image of the old town core. We inspectors need greater authority."
Bystander: "It's a good thing you don't have it ... because you'd probably cause even more damage!"

In the same newspaper we read that "Jakov Brdar [a well-known Slovenian sculptor] is opposed to the erection of sculptures on the 'boulevard' by the railway station. The area between the health insurance building and the soulless blocks of flats, the numerous 'fresh burek

172 Manca Borko, "Za Plečnika jim ni mar" [They Don't Give a Damn about Plečnik], *Delo*, December 2, 2004, 6.

173 Mateja Gruden, "Vse je (bilo) narobe, nihče ni ukrepal" [Everything Is (Was) Wrong, [but] Nobody Did Anything about It], *Delo*, December 11, 2003, 7.

174 Boris Jukič, three-frame comic strip, *Delo*, July 18, 2005, 18.

daily' signs, etc., cannot be the home to a horseman for whom the artist has envisaged a more intimate and noble mission—a place of gathering and connecting."[175] A bronze equestrian statue as a place of gathering and connecting? Isn't that what a burek is, or a burekkiosk with a sign that reads "fresh burek daily"?

Of course, some of the above cases could also refer to the sloppiness, inappropriateness, and lack of aesthetic appeal of these burek stands, as writer Dušan Merc described the Slovenian stands at the Frankfurt book fair: "The Slovenian stands are burek stands."[176] But on the other hand it seems that in many of the above statements it is not just a problem involving solely the burek's foreignness or non-indigenousness; the burek's lack of refinement, sloppiness, and worthlessness, etc., are probably also at work here. Therefore the discourses and meanings frequently overlap and it only rarely seems that the dictatorship of a single and sole discourse predominates. One would much more often be likely to find an alliance of several discourses. And that alliance is never concluded just in particular fields (for instance, in the appropriation of place), but are found across the entire enunciative field.

From the appropriation of place, or better the burekalizing of place, let's move to the burekalizing of language. In the nineties, and perhaps earlier, the burek entered the lexicons of slang ("you're a burek"), comparison ("you look like a burek") and elsewhere. The negative connotations that the burek has in the stylistic figures of the Slovene language are the opposite of those which it has in Bosnia and Herzegovina, land of the burek numero uno, where it is associated with home, warmth, safety and sociability.[177] And of course here, as in many places before,

175 Jelka Šutej Adamič, "Meso, žganje in divja etno glasba" [Meat, Spirits and Wild Ethno Music], *Delo, Sobotna priloga*, February 27, 1999, 40.

176 Dušan Merc, "Sit sem vseh teh tujcev" [I'm Sick of All these Foreigners], *Večer, Sobotna priloga*, January 20, 2001, 33.

177 The burek has a high status in the nutritional ideology of Bosnia and Herzegovina, and also primarily among other Muslim populations in the Balkans, in Turkey and also in various Arabic countries. Among Muslims in Bosnia and Herzegovina it is considered a staple food, like bread. The burek and other pies in Bosnia and Herzegovina and elsewhere in the Balkans and in Turkey are of course not just family dishes. But there are significant differences between burekstands in Slovenia and burekstands in Bosnia and Herzegovina and elsewhere in the Balkans. First of all what they are called. In Bosnia and Herzegovina and in certain other countries which have appeared on the territory of the former SFRY they are called "buregdžinicas," while in Slovenia there is no

and later as well, we find ourselves confronted with the standard, unavoidable problem in the social sciences, the problem of meaning. For whom do these stylistic figures have meaning? And of course, what kind of meaning? In *Razvezani jezik* [Twisted Tongue], the free (online) dictionary of living Slovene, under "burek" we find the following interpretation of the above phraseme:

> *In colloquial language, burek also means an idiot or an incompetent. For example:* "Ste pa res eni bureki!" *[You're a bunch of complete bureks!] Of course within this derogatory use of the word lies a more or less hidden chauvinistic or racist component; burek in this sense implies a slow-witted and incompetent southerner, a Balkan, or an Oriental.*[178]

But the majority of users of this phraseme are not aware of this "more or less hidden chauvinistic or racist component." Without delving too deeply into this debate, I should point out that despite the fact that the majority of users of this phraseme and other figures of speech are not aware of their nationalist impulse, some kind of nationalist discourse is at work in the enunciation. Whether these users are aware of how they themselves interpret it (if at all), and what its real consequences are, are of course other questions which shall not be addressed here.

Thus what has occurred is the appearance of new collocations, compounds, and derivatives, in which we might find the teeth marks of a ravenous nationalist discourse, i.e. the jaws of burekalism. In the second act of the radio play *Klinika Tivoli d.o.o.* [Tivoli Clinic Inc.], which was broadcast on Radio Slovenija in 1992, Dr. Kulani, an Albanian from Kosovo and a specialist at the institution in question, is driven out by the Ljubljana "burek mafia," which wants him to give them a recipe for dough for an "ultramodern burek," from which Act II also got its name ("The Recipes of

---

special name for them, and in contrast with buregdžinicas they also frequently offer "pleskavica" meat patties, hamburgers, pizza, kebabs, and other fast food in addition to bureks. A lot of Slovenian burekstands also do not have seating areas. So at Slovenian burekstands, bureks are usually served wrapped in paper and are eaten without silverware, while in the buregdžinicas they are served on a plate and eaten with forks.

178 Anon., accessed March 10, 2007, http://razvezanijezik.org/?page=burek.

Dr. Kulani"), and threatens to blow up the clinic if they don't get the recipe. Of course they get it, and after a few days of working at the clinic Dr. Kulani is promoted to heart surgeon.[179] A tag to a humorous article with Slovenian-Serbian political motifs in the "Toti list" humour supplement to the Slovenian daily, *Večer*, reads "*Burekolozno*" [i.e. burekalous], a pun on the Slovene word for scandalous.[180] In colloquial, more or less nationalistically and chauvinistically tinged language the expression "burekmajstri" [burekmasters] is used narrowly to denote Albanians, i.e. for Slovenes the best-known and most visible producers of bureks, and broadly to denote all other immigrants from the former SFRY.[181]

And from the appropriation of language further to the issue of eating/not eating bureks. This strange partnership of not/consuming bureks and nationalist discourse slightly eludes this analysis. Of course I could offer numerous stories and statements under this heading. I will present just one. Aida Kurtović, for many years a journalist at Slovenia's main alternative radio station Radio Študent, hosted a show from 1989 to 1991 called "Balkan urnebes" (urnebes is a pepper-based Serbian spread, which means "disorder" or "mess" in colloquial language) and from 1991 to 1997 a show called "Nisam ja odavde" [I'm Not From Here] (in Serbo-Croatian). On one of her shows in December 1991, she conducted an interview with the leading Slovenian nationalist Zmago Jelinčič in Serbo-Croatian. During the show she invited him to the first "Balkan party" at the popular K4 club and thus also for burek, which they

179 Lojze Smasek, "Posmehljivka v nadaljevanjih" [A Comedy in Several Acts], *Večer*, June 12, 1992, 6.

180 Anon., "Doći ćemo po ono struju i sendviče!!!" [We're Coming for Electricity and Sandwiches!!! [in Serbo-Croatian]], *Večer*, January 12, 1999, 41.

181 This is a case of the simplest form of the relationship between food and ethnic and/or nationalist identity, encapsulated in the expression "you are what you eat," which is frequently used to designate "others" (i.e. Slovenes call Italians "Makaronarji," meaning, "macaroni eaters"). We can find many similar examples among various ethnic and national groups in various historical periods. The English, for instance, called the Irish "potato people" in the 19th century, northern Italians called Sicilians "Macaroni eaters" in the 16th century, the French today call the Italians "Macaroni," the Belgians "Fried potato eaters," the English "Roast beef," the French are called "Frogs" by the English, etc. (Peter Scholliers, "Meals, Food Narratives, and Sentiments of Belonging in Past and Present", in *Food, Drink and Identity in Europe Since the Middle Ages*, ed. Peter Scholliers [Oxford; New York: Berg, 2001], 4). In this context I should give the example of an Albanian family from the small Slovenian town of Kidričevo, who were called "bureks" by the locals, even though the family in question was engaged in the sale of fruit, vegetables, and ice cream (Goran Forbici, conversation, winter, 2007).

were handing out at the door. Jelinčič's response to the invitation (for a burek) was: "From your hands I would even eat the Devil."[182] The story was reported in the humour column "Rolanje po sceni" [Roller-skating through the Scene] in the weekly magazine *Mladina*: "Before New Year, Zmago Jelinčić together with his countrymen attended a Balkan party at K-4 (he ate burek from Aida Kurtović's hands press)."[183] And from this entertaining but meaningful story to the questions which it poses, although perhaps indirectly. Nationalist discourse and eating bureks create complex and not entirely clear relations and pose complex questions: How and to what extent do these negative connotations of the burek influence its consumption? Have the nationalists and everyone who has in one way or another joined this discourse eaten bureks? (Recall the statement above: "at least someone agrees with me... but I still like bureks anyhow.")[184] And if they did, how did they eat them? In secret or in public, with a bad conscience or without, did they tell nationalist jokes while doing so or did they realize that bureks are something which is actually not worth discriminating against?

Actually, these are not questions for this particular analysis, so I will answer with a somewhat unusual response, in fact a story, a mixture of enunciation and silence. The makers of bureks undoubtedly did not want their product to become a subject of discrimination. Their strategies for avoiding discrimination were different, but on the other hand, very similar. Similar in that they tried to separate the burek from the semantic associations with the Balkans, the South, and immigrants, and bring it closer to other associations which for Slovenes are more highly valued meanings and elements; this has been the operative strategy of Albanian sweetshop operators for many decades (e.g. sweetshops bearing the names of "sacred" Slovenian places such as Triglav, Soča, etc.). Thus we actually never find a burekstand with a name that would in any way signify or indicate the place where this dish is most widespread or from which its sellers come, which of course is not at all the

182 Aida Kurtović, conversation, June, 2005.

183 Anon., "Rolanje po sceni" [Roller-skating through the Scene], *Mladina*, January 14, 1992, 11.

184 Niet, accessed September 15, 2006, http://www.sloport.net/forum/viewthread.php?tid=-5920&page=5#neprebrano.

case for shops selling other ethnic foods. In this respect a partial exception to this rule is the fast food chain called "Eurobalkan," which on the other hand could also reflect a certain perversion of the dominant, i.e. burekalist, discourse. We also find a total avoidance of statements of the origin, traditional areas or territories importing bureks into Slovenia on packaging or in the advertisements of mass producers of bureks. This silence is especially telling in view of the fact that both industrial mass producers of bureks do not do the same with certain of their other products (for instance, all packaging for various types of croissants invariably has the adjective "French" juxtaposed to the noun). To this euphoric flight towards Europe I can add a recipe for "euroburek" (a pie with spinach, meat and cheese),[185] and for "a little more SLO and veggie, and mushrooms for a change," which hides beneath the telling title "Da burek ne bo Turek" [So that the burek won't be a Turk].[186] Perhaps we should not read this recipe as flirting with Europe, but as an ironic statement about such unseemly coquetry. But who's to know?

From appropriation of consumption just for a moment, really just a moment, to production. In fact, to business. And only just enough so that we can arrive at the title for the next subchapter. So, a short excerpt from an article on the Angua mega-food fair in Cologne, which included an exhibition by the Pekarna Pečjak bakery, which "has an opportunity on the German market with bureks, and not with *kifeljci* [jelly rolls, a dish which Slovenes consider to be "theirs"], popovers and other products from the modern factory."[187] So, some excerpts from an article whose semantics make its self-evidence less clear, but whose syntax confirms it:

Slovenes into Europe with Bureks

I will allow myself a bit of hypothesizing, such as arises from the unique historical contradictoriness of the commercial decisions of the Pečjak bakery. The following section will be somewhat dedicated to

185 Matevž Šalehar, "Prvi Evrogrižljaj" [First Eurobite], *Večer*, May 7, 2004, 57.

186 Matevž Šalehar, "Da burek ne bo Turek" [So that the Burek Won't Be a Turk], *Večer*, January 23, 2004, 57.

187 Marjeta Šoštarič, "Slovenci z burekom v Evropo" [Slovenes into Europe with Bureks], *Delo*, October 17, 2003, 4.

burekeaters. In particular a group of burekeaters which clearly and to a large degree had an influence on the popularization and visibility of the burek, and which also indirectly had influence on the fact that for Pekarna Pečjak and also for the majority of Slovenian bakeries, the burek became "item number one in Slovenia," as it was succinctly described by a technician at the bakery,[188] and which then led to those commercial decisions and the title of this section. But the apparently unimportant adverb "indirectly" in the above utterance carries a great deal of weight in this hypothesis. This group of Slovene burekeaters, which influenced its popularization and visibility, in my view actually primarily ate "non-domestic" bureks. Therefore, let's explore the background of this somewhat or even quite improper hypothesis.

Numerous conversations with youth during the nineties bear witness to how the burek very quickly became a popular and even revered food among young urbanites, college and secondary-school students.[189] Although it is very difficult to shed sufficient light on the complex relationship between this burekloving discourse and burekconsumption, it is not difficult to recognize the socio-cultural background to that relationship.

Peter Stankovič says that a rebellious spirit began to spread mainly among the urban youth who expressed ambivalence towards the project of Slovenian independence. Of course we can ask ourselves about the relative significance of being indifferent towards Slovenia's independence and how much rebellious spirit there actually was.[190] But

188 Technician at Pečjak bakery, telephone conversation, June 19, 2006.

189 Cristina Hardyment (cited in David Bell and Gill Valentine, *Consuming Geographies: We Are Where We Eat* [London; New York: Routledge, 1997], 173–174) in a description of ethnic food in England claims that students were the main culprits for the popularization of Indian and Chinese food in the sixties, primarily owing to their affordability and exoticness. And from there to a quick jaunt through Slovenian history. Maja Godina Golija writes on eating habits in Maribor during the interwar period: "the biggest consumers of hot meals on the streets were young people, mainly secondary-schoolers, who were able to get a quick hot meal this way." (*Prehrana v Mariboru v dvajsetih in tridesetih letih 20. Stoletja* [Eating Habits in Maribor in the Nineteen-Twenties and Thirties] [Maribor: Založba Obzorja, 1996], 126.) This is in fact all that I was able to find on the history of the eating habits of college and secondary-school students in Slovenia in the professional and scientific literature. And what of the hungry Ivan Cankar, Dragotin Kette, Josip Murn, and numerous other great Slovene writers? Did anyone care about the empty and growling stomachs of the literati?

190 Stankovič gives as an example of one of the initial manifestations of this rebellious spirit a party which occurred completely spontaneously at the B-51 club on Gerbičeva street in Ljubljana on the

let's leave such questions aside for the moment. Whatever it was, it was expressed through enthusiasm for all things Balkan and southern. This was in fact not a political movement, Stankovič continues, but it brought about an interesting cultural inversion, in which part of the urban youth (primarily college students, alternative-lifestyle proponents and secondary-schoolers) changed everything Balkan from a symbol of the bad into a symbol of the good. Thus, it was a deviation that was opposed to the "official" dominant discourse:

> *Overnight, so-called "Balkan parties" became immensely popular, pop and rock music from former Yugoslavia started to "rule"; even for those who were too young to hear it as they grew up, the use of Serbo-Croatian as slang became unbelievably popular, bureks and baklava became the height of fashion, well-known Serbian comedies (Ko to tamo peva [Who's Singin' Over There?], Maratonci [The Marathon Family], Balkanski spijun [Balkan Spy], Kako je propao rokenrol [The Fall of Rock and Roll], etc.) became references which everyone had to know, in short, a certain nostalgic sentiment spread like wildfire among the urban youth, which probably more than anything else expressed a fear that life in independent Slovenia would become too "Austrian": too closed, narrow-minded, puritanical and blinkered.*[191]

Or as Boris Čibej historically analyzes his love for bureks: "[A]t the beginning of the 80s, when nobody ever dreamed that the nation would fall apart, we were also unable to have any Yugonostalgia, which most likely led to our later love of bureks[.]"[192] To summarize: the post-independence youths' and also others' love for bureks is associated with a

---

very day of the proclamation of Slovenia's independence, 15 June 1991: "At the moment when all of Slovenia was rejoicing in its secession from Yugoslavia, a crowd of young people danced and drank all night to the nostalgic sounds of Yugo rock (i.e. Yugoslavian rock music), and at the end danced a ring dance to the frenzied rhythms of Serbian nationalists." (Peter Stankovič, "Rokerji s konca tisočletja" [Rockers at the End of the Millennium], in *Urbana plemena. Subkulture v Sloveniji v devetdesetih* [Urban Tribes: Subcultures in Slovenia in the Nineties], ed. Peter Stankovič, Gregor Tomc, and Mitja Velikonja [Ljubljana: Študentska založba, 1999], 46)

191 Stankovič, "Rokerji s konca tisočletja," 46.

192 Boris Čibej, e-mail message to author, April 2, 2005.

certain nostalgia, which at least in certain segments can be understood as a more or less implicit rebellion against the dominant popular and also the predominant official discourse in the newly-formed country. David Bell and Gill Valentine state that the fear of foreign foods and their threat to national projects also always contains an element of reverence or even fetishization owing to their (exotic) otherness, which adds, to use a bit of culinary jargon, a bit of spice to life. The history of food tells us stories about both xenophobia and neophilia, veneration and rejection, i.e., both dictatorships and...[193]

Particularly among the younger urban population, among college and secondary-school students, the burek, according to Stankovič, increasingly began to function as a signifier of something cool and also began to carry other meanings of the South and the Balkans.[194] These alternative burekmeanings, which were more or less diametrically opposed to the nationalistic discourse, would probably be very difficult to designate as an explicit rebellion against nationalism. So it was probably more of an alternative rather than an oppositional discourse, although the line between them, as Raymond Williams said, is often undetectable.[195]

One of the first articulations of this alternative discourse is the burek that was handed out as an entrance ticket to the first "Balkan party" at the K4 club in Ljubljana at the end of December 1991. Before this they had distributed bureks on November 29 at the second "Balkan party" at the B-51 club. At the first "Balkan party" at the B-51 club (May 24, 1991), upon buying their tickets at the door, the guests also received a shot of *rakija* (fruit brandy popular in southern Slavic countries), and once inside Serbian cheese, onions and bread. At the second party the

193 Bell and Valentine, *Consuming Geographies*, 165.

194 Peter Stankovič, "Burek? Ja, bitte!" 36–37.

195 Williams, "Base and Superstructure," 42. The difference between the alternative and the oppositional is a difference, to use Williams' words, "between someone who simply finds a different way to live and wishes to be left alone with it, and someone who finds a different way to live and wants to change society in its light" (Ibid.). On one hand therefore we are talking about political passivity and on the other about political engagement in practices which represent a form of competition against or deviation from the dominant forms. This difference, undoubtedly useful for our study, is however a strict one, and that strictness is in the final analysis also antitheoretical: isn't forming definitions about whether a cultural activity is alternative or oppositional merely my own stance?

guests were served *pasulj* (a traditional Serbian bean dish) and bureks, which were made by the aforementioned Aida Kurtović.[196]

Actually, the most common statement in this oppositional discourse was eating the burek itself. If I may be allowed to indulge in some of my burekmemories from my college years, mainly from the mid-nineties on, when more than once a week partying at so-called Balkan parties and other college parties (at which "yugo" music played a featured role) nearly always ended with a burek at the Ljubljana bus station. Going out for a burek was, as confirmed by numerous other partiers of the era and later, almost a ritual conclusion to a night of partying.

In this debate about the consumption of bureks we have to remember—and I would like to particularly emphasize this—the isolated position of the burek within the range of fast food and particularly within the food that was available extremely late at night. I believe it is at least too narrow, if not actually wrong, to see the burek merely as a symbolic object which college students and other youths in the nineties ate simply due to its symbolic weight, its symbolic position—i.e. due to its conceptual association with the South. First of all we have to ask ourselves what was available at the time, of course for not much money, anywhere anytime, and with the possibility of at least a minimal choice (cheese & meat). Students and other youths in the nineties did not eat bureks primarily because they were Balkan, southern, because they represented a rebellion against the dominant discourse; but mainly because they were cheap, filling, available anywhere anytime and because, at least for me, they sat wonderfully on an alcohol-filled stomach. If it had been primarily about symbols, students would probably have chosen čevapčiči,[197] which at least at the end of the eighties were a more symbolically charged dish than bureks—they came up, at least in my selective overview of various materials from those times—more

---

196 Igor Bašin, conversation, June 7, 2005, and telephone conversation, March 24, 2006.

197 Čevapčiči most likely have a somewhat longer history in Slovenia than bureks. Isolated examples of sellers of čevapčiči and ražnjiči, which at the time were called "turške klobasice" [little Turkish sausages] appeared on the streets of some Slovenian towns in the 1930s (see Janez Bogataj, "Hitra prehrana – dediščina in sodobnost" [Fast Food – Heritage and Modernity], in *Hitra hrana* [Fast Food], ed. Dražigost Pokorn [Ljubljana: Inštitut za higieno, MF, 1997], 15). Maja Godina Golija, in her study of eating habits in Maribor between the two world wars writes that the first seller of čevapčiči and ražnjiči appeared in the town in 1933. (*Prehrana v Mariboru*, 126.)

often when searching for Juga, Balkan, and southerners. This story about burekeaters in the nineties has to be approached from another direction.

Burekeating was often accompanied by other burekloving activities. Consumption, especially the consumption of such semantic charged things as bureks, is not an isolated, unique phenomenon, but is embedded in a network of other associations and activities. Simon Stojko Falk remembers what he calls a "film scene" from the mid-nineties of a spontaneous gathering of youths waiting in line for a burek at night at a kiosk on Miklošičeva street in Ljubljana, loudly singing rapper Ali En's hit *Sirni & mesni* [Cheese & Meat] (i.e. bureks).[198] Damir Josipovič, a former classmate at the Geography Department at the Faculty of Arts of the University of Ljubljana, recalls visiting one of the burekkiosks after a concert. Damir's cohorts joked with the seller, pretending to be Albanians. The seller believed them and a long exchange followed; the group only gradually realized that the seller was not in fact Albanian as they had at first believed.[199]

Undoubtedly we could stretch this alternative discourse to cover all burekloving practices, which would also include burek-making. I will give just one example. Goran Krstić, for whom, as he states himself, the burek "means a lot," makes them "because if there were no bureks on earth, I could make one [...] myself. And a good one." He learned how to make them from a friend's mother, who is Bosnian. They made three bureks (cheese, meat and spinach), first her, then him, then the last one together. He also "wrote everything down, and it wasn't long" before he tried to make one by himself at home. Goran—otherwise a financial consultant, who I met during a celebration of Ramadan in Jesenice; both of us had been invited by the Muslim community—takes three hours or more to make a burek. He is of course very proud of his burekmaking skills, often offers bureks to his family and friends, and shares his knowledge with those who are interested. And he loves to talk about bureks.[200]

198 Simon Stojko Falk, conversation, summer, 2005.
199 Damir Josipovič, telephone conversation, April 2, 2007.
200 Goran Krstić, conversation, autumn, 2006, and e-mail message to author, April 30, 2007.

The background to this antinationalistic discourse, however, can in no way be limited to a nostalgic recollection and/or adulation of the southern/Balkan. The making of affirmative burekstatements is not limited to any "Yugonostalgia" or "Balkannostalgia." Actually, it would be reasonable to divide this affirmative discourse into non-nationalist—which can mean a lot of things, so let's rather call it implicit or alternative—and on the other hand antinationalist, i.e. explicit and oppositional discourse. Therefore, explicit, politically engaged statements would fall into the latter category, while the former would include those for which it would be difficult to say that that's what they actually are. One can see that this implicit discourse at least to a certain extent overlaps with a form of burekloving discourse which is significantly formed and represented by burekeaters. In the case of explicit, oppositional discourse the authors' eating of bureks very rarely, if ever, appears in the statements. The burek is not an object of reverence in and of itself, but is merely a signifier for something, merely stands for something else. Something which has a subordinate position within the existing power relations, which demonstrates a lack of power. Something—and by "something" I mean the thing the burek signifies, and not the burek per se—that seems worth fighting for. Of course such a division can be problematic, since the line between the explicit and the implicit, between the oppositional and the alternative, as we have said above, is often blurred. But isn't this a problem with almost all divisions?

The difference between these two discourses also appears in the actual causes and origins of burekmanifestation. If the burek appears in the implicit discourse primarily due to its unique position within the range of foods available at the time (price, availability) and secondarily because of its associations with the South and the Balkans, it arrived in the explicit discourse more indirectly—via nationalistic discourse. That is to say, the explicit discourse is clearly, explicitly, purposefully antinationalistic. And it was nationalistic discourse—and I hope I have made this sufficiently clear—that was the first to take an uncompromising bite into the burek. Antinationalistic, explicit and of course also nonnationalistic, implicit discourses are merely trying to rescue the burek from this voracious maw.

An article by a well-known columnist with the burekunfriendly title of "A Burek for Jelinčič" [the head of the Slovenian Nationalist Party] is a clear example of this political battle, this explicit discourse. But on the other hand the burek's role, and its location, appearing only at the end (and in the title) is a bit unusual:

> *There are inhibitions which have to exist: people are born equal, people are brothers and sisters, brothers and sisters help each other out. Anyone who dismisses them is preparing the ground for racism, and such people should have their mouths shut. Even if only with a burek.*[201]

So, a burek as a gag for a (proto)racist mouth.

An equally unambiguous discourse, but with the burek more clearly in the role of signifier, appears in a commentary by another well-established journalist, this time with the kajmakunfriendly title of "Landing in Kajmak":

> *And lastly: this type of cleansing has never stopped at the first cases. When Slovenia is free of Serbs, it will be time for the Shiptars, and the Bosnians, and the Roma... all the way to domestic traitors. Then in the ethnically, culturally, and perhaps even racially clean state, patriotism will begin with love for blood sausage with cabbage, žganci and strudel, and end with hatred for everything not Slovene. Who should not be afraid that we will have to hide it from our children and neighbours if we all of a sudden crave a burek, baklava or CDs by the band Mizar?*[202]

If we were to compare a larger number of statements, we would find that the burek hangs out with more or less the usual subjects; in the final analysis it appears within a relatively limited group of signifiers, i.e. paradigms. We find it hand in hand with baklava, čevapčiči, various kinds of Yugo music, and vis-à-vis, or perhaps comparing strength with,

---

201 Marko Crnkovič, "Burek za Jelinčiča" [A Burek for Jelinčič], *Naši razgledi*, August 14, 1992, 477.

202 Dejan Pušenjak, "Desant na kajmak" [Landing in Kajmak], *Večer*, August 12, 1991, 8.

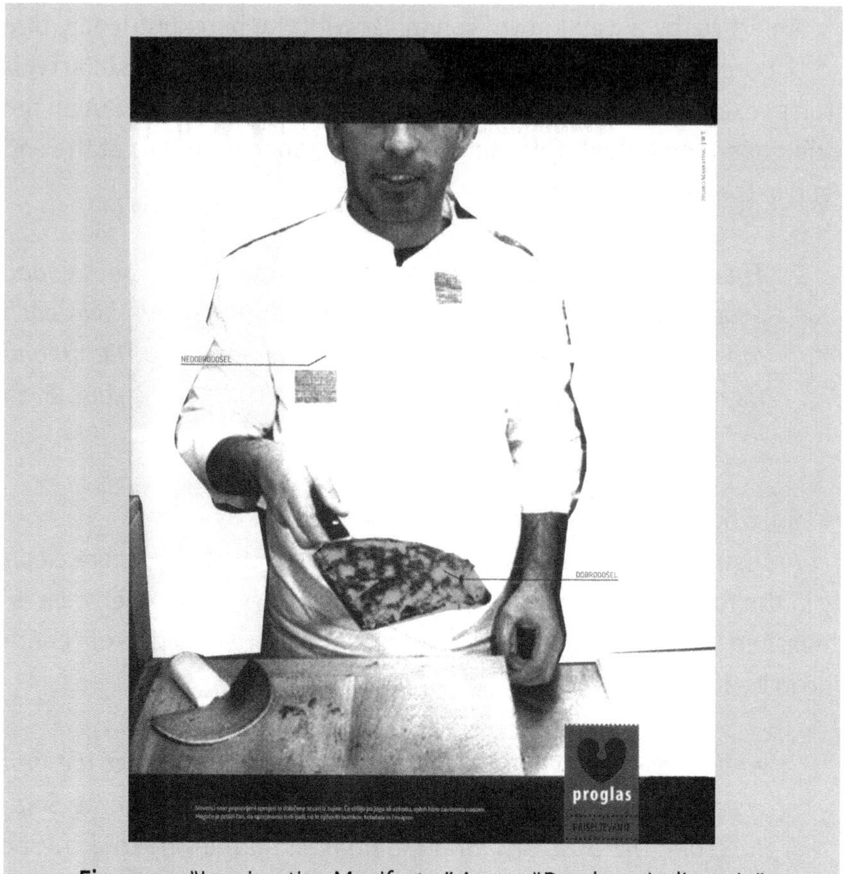

Figure 10. "Immigration Manifesto." Anon., "Proglas priseljevanje" [Immigration Manifesto], *Mladina*, January 23, 2006, 1. Courtesy of *Mladina*.

Carniolan sausage, strudel and beef soup. But of course this burekparadigm, this company of burekallies and burekopponents, also changes slightly over time, as we can conclude from the still-fresh "Immigration Manifesto" in *Mladina*, with captions depicting a burek as "welcome" and a person holding and clearly selling a burek as "unwelcome," and a text in the lower black margin which reads: "We Slovenes are prepared to accept only certain things from abroad. If they smell of the South or the East, we quickly turn up our noses. Perhaps the time has come to accept the people, and not just their bureks, kebabs and čevaps."[203]

203 Anon., "Proglas priseljevanje" [The Immigration Manifesto], *Mladina*, January 23, 2006, 1.

And we can also discover in these affirmative burekstatements a certain similarity, a repetition of a syntagm. Alongside the above syntagm and in opposition to the graffito "Burek? Nein danke" let's juxtapose yet another highly purposeful graffito, which similarly did not end its career only on the town walls. We also find it on websites, and even in the title of a topic on the portal for students at the University of Ljubljana called Student Info, which develops into a very long and polemical debate about immigrants, tolerance and foreigners,[204] and appears in a photo album of Ljubljana graffiti, and probably elsewhere as well: "Yes to bureks but no to mosques, eh?"[205]

Figure 11. "Yes to bureks but no to mosques, eh?"
Photo by Dušan Jež. Courtesy of Dušan Jež.

---

204 Sandra Prajnić, accessed July 13, 2006, http://www.student-info.net/portal/portal.php?stran=prva&vs=novice&id=173. The title is slightly changed here: "Burek bi, a đamije ne, a?" [Yes to bureks but no to mosques, eh?]. This text can also be found at the beginning of one of the topics on the ObalaNET website.

205 Dušan Jež, *Grafiti Ljubljane* [The Graffiti of Ljubljana] (Ljubljana: Noviforum, 2005).

The last three or four statements could be described as explicitly oppositional.[206] They are therefore a part of a group of representations which in a very conscious and engaged manner address the problem of the dominant discourse of representation and the existing power relations or social relations of power.

Of course, the range of strategies of affirmative burekstatements is limited. With the inestimable assistance of Stuart Hall[207] we discover that there is an entire series of statements in which the burek apparently retains its ascribed, stereotypical meanings, but which are no longer understood exclusively and negatively, but approvingly and positively.[208] Probably one example of such a policy of inversion of meaning is the burek which was served at the "Balkan parties," as are numerous names and appellations such as *Stripburek*, Burek teater,[209] etc.

We can additionally recognize affirmative discourse not burdened with Slovene stereotypes, about the burek as "cool, awesome, dude!" which at least in the case of burekstatements is usually manifested more implicitly, such as in various phrasemes ("You don't have enough [money] for a burek"),[210] in the singing of the song *Sirni & mesni* in front of the burekkiosk on Miklošičeva street, in the "Slovene" manner of making bureks or in the following email, sent to "Dr Burek," which owing to its uplifting content, which takes an optimistic view of the proverbially impossible Slovenian political scene, I reprint in its entirety:

> *Hi!*
> *Last week at the Permanent Representation of the Republic of Slovenia to the EU in Brussels, where I currently work, a book called Historical and Cultural Perspectives on Slovenian Migration*

---

206 We could also speak about explicitly antihegemonic statements. But I would prefer not to involve a different terminology, which also has a complex theoretical background.

207 See: Hall, "The Spectacle of the 'Other.'"

208 I should add that I have used and recycled Hall's analysis of (alternative) representations of black skin (Hall, "The Spectacle of the 'Other,'"272–275) somewhat freely, which of course does not mean that any credit for originality devolves to me.

209 From 2005 on also Društvo Burek teater [The Burek Theater Association].

210 Or the memorable photo of strikers with a sign that read "Nimam za burek" [I don't have enough (money) for a burek], Toni Dugorepec, photo, in Jure Aleksič, "Rdeči November" [Red November], *Mladina*, November 23, 2007, 46.

was waiting on my desk. Today I read your article about the burek which was published in it with eager satisfaction, like eating a good burek.
I decided to write this email mainly to compliment the chef. Since I noticed in the blurb at the end of the book that you were writing a book on the subject, I decided to add a suggestion—that it would be let's say interesting to include the female perspective on this matter, since in my experience the art of making bureks is becoming an increasingly important part of the cooking skills of middle-class women, where the greatest success is achieved by those who can make fun of "Fata" [a stereotype for a Bosnian woman, a leading character in stereotypical Bosnian jokes]—and then after searching for your address I found that you had already received your doctorate, and therefore had in all likelihood given up any attempts in this direction.
But I have another suggestion: at the end of our Presidency, we will be inviting our colleagues, cultural consultants to Member States of the EU and other similar EU officials, i.e. those who are responsible for intercultural dialogue, to lunch at the Slovenia House. It would be great if before the event we could send your article together with the invitation, and serve bureks at the event itself.
May I ask you for an electronic copy and your permission to do this?
I hope we have the chance to meet some time,
Sašo[211]

We could also discover certain procedures of destabilization of various critical points through which stereotypical burekrepresentations and burekstatements operate. These include e.g. the "Immigration Manifesto,"[212] the graffito and syntagm "YES TO BUREKS BUT NO TO MOSQUES, EH?"[213] and the Mladina photo collage with the group

211 Sašo Gazdič, e-mail message to author, April 20, 2008.
212 Anon., "Proglas priseljevanje."
213 Jež, *Grafiti Ljubljane*; and Prajnić, July 13, 2006, http://www.student-info.net/portal/portal.php?stran=prva&vs=novice&id=173.

of striking immigrants, one of whom is holding a sign that reads "NO MOSQUE FOR US, NO BUREK FOR YOU."[214]

Of course it is difficult to draw the line between these strategies of affirmative burekstatements. They are often, if not in fact always, inseparably connected. Thus such divisions, at least in my case, can be seen as more of a sort of non-dogmatic insight into the diversity of alternative statement-making than an attempt at classifying them.

In opposition to the graffito "Burek? Nein danke" let's place a text by culturologist Peter Stankovič entitled "Burek? Ja, bitte!" The text is meaningful among other things because its author represents a field which is accorded special weight: science! It is true that the article was published in the Saturday supplement to one of Slovenia's daily newspapers, and that it was therefore written for a wide circle of readers. But on the other hand it is equipped with several additions, decorations and filigrees which the author and the text introduce into the consecrated world of science. For instance, the author's name is adorned with the title of "Dr."—and this ornament is not found only at the beginning, i.e. before the title and all that follows, but also concludes the text ("Doc. dr." [Docent doctor]). In the body of the text the author cites other scientific authorities (e.g. Pierre Bourdieu) and the same text was also published on the website of the Department of Culturology at the Faculty of Social Sciences of the University of Ljubljana, on a page entitled "Monthly Column of Critical Theory of Culture."[215] So let's have a look at how a man of science concludes a text written for a non-scientific audience:

> *In this sense it is possible to understand the burek, at least in one segment, as a symbol of the contribution of the culture of other Yugoslav republics to the civilizing of Slovenia: the culture of the majority of the former republics is also a culture of cities, real cities, dense, large, unpleasant and cold, but at the same time spiritually broad, open, and diverse, and if this urban culture (civilization?) came to Slovenia with the immigrants, if through nothing*

214 Anon., photo montage, in Berto Ritotreb, "Mladinamit," *Mladina*, January 12, 2004, 72.
215 Peter Stankovič, spring, 2007, http://www.fdv-kulturologija.si/kulturologija_kolumna.htm#Burek.

> *else through the food which urban flexibility makes possible, it is not just that nothing was lost through the immigration of "Bosnians" (as implied by Slovene popular nationalistic discourse, as well as the occasional politician), but that Slovenia also gained a great deal through it. So, a burek, then? Ja, bitte!*[216]

To these in one way or another scientifically-supported antinationalistic statements I could also add a paper I wrote, which can be found in the COBISS system under the category "original scientific article," with the somewhat exhausting and (excessively) long title "Slovenes into Europe with Bureks and/or the Dictatorship of the Carniolan Sausage: some thoughts on the burek, representations of the burek and 'Slovene' ethnonational discourse," which was published in the journal *Dve domovini/Two Homelands.*[217] So let's have a look at how a man of science concludes a text written for a scientific audience:

> *And in fact the burek also propelled us into Europe. To a much greater extent than the Carniolan sausage. In 2004 an article on Slovenia in the British newspaper* The Guardian *proclaimed the burek as the Slovenian national dish. They later corrected the error, so that in the online edition the burek was changed into potica cake [...]. And when Mormon missionary Jordan Cullimore was asked in Jana about the culinary delights of "our beautiful country," he replied, "I'm going to miss Cockta (Slovenian cola), bureks, and Poli salami when I leave." And not a ghost of a whisper about Carniolan sausage!*[218]

---

216 Stankovič, "Burek? Ja, bitte!"

217 Yet another example of the referentiality of statements. The journalist Boris Jež referred to the scientific article from *Dve domovini/Two Homelands* in a column entitled "An Interesting Slice of Heaven" (Boris Jež, "Zanimiv košček nebes" [An Interesting Slice of Heaven], *Delo, Sobotna priloga*, July 15, 2006, 13.), which or a part of which can also be found in the text before you. And similarly in this text you can also find numerous examples of Jež's other texts as well as an excerpt from the article from *Dve domovini/Two Homelands*, which among other things includes a smattering of Jež's texts. (Sic!)

218 Jernej Mlekuž, "Slovenci z burekom v Evropo in/ali diktatura kranjske klobase: Nekaj o bureku, reprezentacijah bureka in 'slovenskem' etnonacionalnem diskurzu" [Slovenes into Europe with Bureks and/or the Dictatorship of the Carniolan Sausage: Some Thoughts on the Burek, Representations of the Burek and 'Slovene' Ethnonational Discourse], *Dve domovini/Two Homelands* 23 (2006): 174.

Utterly frivolous, isn't it?

If we have a look at the preceding story, we can see that science is at one time in cahoots with the dominant discourse and at another on the side of the opposition. First it is the burek's great enemy, and then it's in love with it.

But let's move away from scientific authority into the more freedom-loving, freethinking world of ideas, jokes, wisecracks and other less formalized notions (among which the differences are perhaps not as great as they appear to be). Dan Podjed, my former classmate at the Department of Ethnology and Cultural Anthropology, would like to replace the stars in the European flag with a slice of pizza burek. That is, the pizza burek as a new symbol of the united Europe: "old" Western Europe (pizza) and "new" Eastern Europe (burek). It is, he says, a "fantastic idea" which for now "has traction only in pub debates."[219] So then, into Europe with bureks! But I think that we have arrived at a special type of statements. Statements which deserve special treatment, despite the frivolous title.

A Good Laugh

The division into "The Dictatorship of the Carniolan Sausage" and "With Bureks into Europe," not to mention earlier on into "Greasy Junk Food" and "The Burek is Great"—i.e. into a kind of dominant and exclusive and on the other hand oppositional and alternative, approving, and affirmative discourse[220] is in fact a coarse attempt to grapple with the heterogeneity of statements, a callous, coarse understanding of the complexity of statements, discourses, practices and representations. Moreover, it is also a problematic understanding. Statements can be read very differently; or to put it another way, isn't it possible for statements to support and be included in several even opposing strategies of power and meaning, to reproduce several even opposing discourses?

---

219 Dan Podjed, telephone conversation, February 22, 2007.

220 This division could be partially juxtaposed with Stuart Hall's—familiar in media and cultural studies—division of systems of meaning or ways of decoding messages in the mass media. Hall's division can also help us understand and conceptualize the ambiguity and interpretation of statements.

Figure 12. "Stripburek: comics from behind the rusty iron curtain." Jakob Klemenčič and Marcel Ruijters, in *Stripburek: Comics from Behind the Rusty Iron Curtain*, ed. Katerina Mirović (Forum Ljubljana – Stripburger, Ljubljana, 1997), back cover. Courtesy of Stripburger / Forum Ljubljana.

What for instance would you say about the back cover of a special edition of the comic *Stripburger*, entitled "Stripburek: comics from behind the rusty iron curtain"—i.e. the first anthology of original comic strips from Eastern Europe?

First of all, a none-too-pleasant question arises with regard to the complexity of this statement. How are we supposed to read it? As one, two or more statements? And how are these (sub)statements interconnected? In the first equation the burek is equated to grease underlined, and then even squared, thus bringing to the surface some variety of healthy-lifestyle discourse, such as it is, want it or not. The last equation we can recognize as burekalism, and Edward Said would probably even recognize it as Orientalism. On the connotative level the suspicious, swarthy face in the unkempt burekkiosk could impute a lot of suspicious or evil intent to the sellers of these "Oriental pies" and of course more broadly to the ethnic group to which they belong, and probably to immigrants in general. But it is likely that the choice itself (the burek) suggests that, of course with an understanding of the broader context, the background, the people or groups which stand behind the product, that the burek was not chosen through any nationalistic impulse, but to the contrary, through some, although not necessarily conscious, subversive stance (as subversive as it may be), which does not exclude the burek. Thus on the connotative level the pie also offers a completely different reading in comparison with the above. The burek can be understood as the only warm, human object in a cold, dehumanized post-socialist environment. And when we ask the authors or subscribers about the encoded messages, we often do not get the desired, "right" answer: "We didn't even think about whether some Polish guy would get it. We just wanted some fast food which was made in the south and that's all. [...] We knew that Western Europe wouldn't understand the burek, so we put a definition at the end."[221] We thus have to understand these statements as complex and entangled products, forms which in various ways combine numerous interests, strategies, ideas, influences, intentions, and meanings. How much all of this is recognizable and transparent to the people included in the uttering, how aware they are of the various forces and discourses which frame the statements, and how consciously and intentionally they support the various forces and discourses is another question entirely.

221 Katerina Mirović and Ivan Mitrevski, conversation, summer, 2005.

What, for example, should we say about this image?[222]

Figure 13. "The Slovenian hen is endangered!" Anon., in Tropinovec, "Slovenska kokoška je ogrožena" [The Slovenian Hen is Endangered], *Večer*, December 16, 2004, 41. Courtesy of *Večer*.

I think that there is no real need to continue with this game of dissection, through which I wish to show that statements are not entirely ideologically conformist, that they do not impose uniform or authoritative meanings. And I am not using this polysemy, this porosity of statements to measure only "good laughs"—the statements presented in this subchapter. Many of the statements from the first subchapter, "The Dictatorship of the Carniolan Sausage"—about which we have

222 Anon., photomontage, in Tropinovec, "Slovenska kokoška je ogrožena" [The Slovenian Hen is Endangered], *Večer*, December 16, 2004, 41.

already stated that they support the existing power relations in one way or another—are not (necessarily) unidirectional, uniform or one-dimensional with respect to power. It seems that the majority of statements allow or open a space for various, even completely contrary (with respect to power) interpretations. And there is no real difference for the numerous statements from the second subchapter, "With Bureks into Europe." So we can almost always find cracks in the apparently very solid constructions of reality.

And this, to paraphrase Barthes' metaphor, is not just different types of reading which appear upon the death of the author. The birth of an author's work also includes more than just one idea, one meaning, reflects more than just one power relationship. The question of what an author means by a certain statement is very often irrelevant. Authors often mean very little and sometimes mean nothing at all. So who is doing the meaning for them?

In other words, statements carry meanings, whether their speakers are aware of them or not. And this is not about adding that they always have meaning for somebody. I am saying—to put it simply, without delving into deep theoretical grounds—that something is operating which is not always explicit or transparent. Something which thinks (instead of) us. As Marx would say: "We are not aware of this, nevertheless we do it."[223] And here we are influenced by Louis Althusser's theory of (ideological) interpellation. Individuals are made into subjects by the fact that they respond to (ideological) discourse which operates on them and interpellates them.[224] Thus the individual is always already imagined in discourse (Althusser is of course speaking of ideology). Discourse therefore has to be understood as a kind of "coerced belief," as something which is compelled regardless of the will of those involved, who are thus interpreters, and which operates regardless of whether

223 Marx uses this sentence to explain the relationship between exchange value and abstract human labour. Thus he states: "whenever, by an exchange, we equate as values our different products, by that very act, we also equate, as human labour, the different kinds of labour expended upon them. We are not aware of this, nevertheless we do it." (Karl Marx, *Capital: A Critique of Political Economy. Volume I: The Process of Capitalist Production*, translated from the 3rd German edition, by Samuel Moore and Edward Aveling [Chicago: Charles H. Kerr and Co., 1909], 83)

224 Louis Althusser, "Ideology and Ideological State Apparatuses," in *Lenin and Philosophy and Other Essays*, trans. Ben Brewster (London: New Left Books, 1971).

those who are included, the interpreters, are aware of it or not. Discourse, to borrow Marx's words once more, "does not stalk about with a label describing what it is."[225]

And what should we say about Ali En's hit *Sirni & mesni*?[226] Well, let's ask the artist. Dalaj Eegol, the former Ali En, in response to the question "When you were writing the song, were you aware that the burek also has political, (anti)nationalist connotations and meanings?" said: "I was aware that the song was a good laugh. There was nothing like what you're asking about. My stance in that song was strictly in relation to the burek." And in explanation he sent the song lyrics, which in view of the fact that two thirds were quoted above, I will recite only one third here:

> *If I don't know where to get one, I just run down to the station*
> *And ask my Albanian friend:*
> *You got cheesy you got meaty, make it fast god shake you*
> *Meaty cheesy it don't matter burek burek you delicious thing I eat*
> *Give me a burek a cheese burek a meat burek, for my:*
> *Burek (8 x)*[227]

But in a previous communication, sent to the author just a few days earlier, in response to the question "Did you even eat them back then?" he said:

> *I myself didn't really like them that much. Particularly bought ones. The song was a clear homage to the lifestyle of a certain generation at the time. It obviously stirred up or awakened some sincere feelings among people regarding their attitudes towards the south, which couldn't be expressed in any other way. I thought*

225 "Value, therefore, does not stalk about with a label describing what it is." (Marx, *Capital*, 83)

226 Ali En, *Sirni & mesni*. Many Slovene and of course foreign pop musicians sing about food and play with it in one way or another (but much less often than with sex, drugs, or alcohol). In 2001, Korado and Brendi named both a song and an album Čevapčiči, the band *Srečna mladina* [Happy Youth] called their first album *Tenstan krompir je kul* [Pan-Fried Potatoes are Cool]; cf. the bands *Yogurt*, *Riblja čorba* [Fish Stew], *Bananarama*, Zoran Predin's ode *Pražen krompir* [Fried Potatoes], etc.

227 Dalaj Eegol, e-mail message to author, July 16, 2005.

> *the bureks from the station were tasteless and greasy, and the rest were similar.*[228]

In a third letter, sent to the author nearly a year later, I asked about different content, but in the same manner. I asked, "Was the song at all connected with an ironic or subversive stance towards the very violent debate in the media over healthy lifestyles, healthy food, in which the burek as a grease-laden fast food is ranked very low?" The songwriter replied somewhat testily: "Do you even take life seriously, with questions like that?"; "WHY do you complicate so much?"; "that's not what it was about at the time". But to the next question, "In that song were you trying to joke about that debate about healthy food?" he responded, to the contrary: "I did anyhow, if you didn't notice."[229] So? It's not a very good example, but at any rate in my opinion it shows that during the writing of this song various discourses were at work in very different ways, regardless of how or to what extent its author was aware of them, or wanted to be.

To summarize: only with difficulty can we believe the songwriter's assertion that his "stance in that song was strictly in relation to the burek." Why for instance does he say that he "didn't really like them that much"? We might buy that his "stance was strictly in relation to the burek," but only on the assumption that that burek was never just meant to fill his belly, but other things as well. Many, many other things.

Let's stay with *Sirni & mesni* for a while. Ali En's hit probably at least to some extent also helped to popularize the burek, but also contributed to a (discursive) burekcalming, burekassimilation, burekmainstreamization. The song, which got airplay on almost all of the radio stations in Slovenia for a long time, was probably the most effective marketing and promotional tool the burek ever had. Young people in the second half of the nineties would loudly sing "Burek, burek..." in all sorts of settings—like the "film scene" from that time which I referred to earlier: a group of youths spontaneously singing Ali En's hit while waiting in line for bureks in front of the kiosk on Miklošičeva street in Ljubljana.[230]

---

228 Eegol, e-mail message to author, July 13, 2005.

229 Eegol, e-mail message to author, May 27, 2006.

230 Simon Stojko Falk, conversation, summer, 2005.

The kids who sang "Burek, burek..." in front of the kiosk probably also quite unconsciously used the phraseme "you're a burek," and thus reproduced burekalism. The burek, so to speak, had both a good and a bad reputation. At least some of those youths simultaneously communicated, maintained and constituted both discourses, both the nationalistic and the antinationalistic, both the dominant and the alternative/oppositional. The burek was labelled with both affirmative, approving and positive meanings and dismissive, negative, excluding ones, with very different nuances on a palette ranging from the unaware, unreflective and self-evident on one end to the engaged, conscious and reflective on the other.

A complex ambivalence, then, which can also be seen as a consistent ambivalence. It tells us that with or through the burek, we are all oppressed and at the same time all oppressors. And we are these things in very different, complex ways, without being aware of it at all. With or through the burek we are thus involved in diverse and complex power relations. And we are variously crossed, cut, touched, tickled, grazed or stabbed. Sometimes it hurts us, sometimes we like it, sometimes we don't even know it's happening, and sometimes we write a doctoral thesis about it.

Making an analysis of these complex and diverse attitudes and styles is, in my humble opinion, a false errand from its inception, which can never be satisfyingly, accurately, sufficiently or clearly completed. We can only try to trace the complexity and diversity of the statements and their complex inclusion in the fields of signification and power. Each interpretation is already in its essence incomplete, often even highly questionable and problematic, and in the best case only a partial project. As we have said elsewhere, interpretations never produce final, absolute truths. So if we finally accept the necessity of the interpretive nature of culture, we must accept that we are unavoidably trapped in a continuous process of discarding and searching for meaning.

Interpretation can, at least from a more bleak perspective, only burden us with additional and ever newer tasks, thus always removing us further from a conclusion, from an end to our work. But from another, more positive perspective, it shines forth as the only tool we have in this project of delineating the complexity, diversity, and entanglement of statements and their complex inclusion in the fields of signification and power.

Before we leave this magic circle of interpretation and searching for meanings, let's take a look at a few examples which will shed additional light on this continuous discarding of meaning, this interpretive behaviour, reminiscent of pushing Sisyphus' rock up the hill, and on the other hand of the usefulness of this universal unique and fundamental human tool, without which man would be merely a natural phenomenon, if anything at all. So let's look at this behaviour, which inescapably accompanies social facts and is itself also a social fact, from both the pleasant and the unpleasant perspectives.

In the low-budget Slovenian film *Tu pa tam* [Here and There], Ortič, a descendant of immigrants from the south, who parades around throughout the entire film in the uniform of the (Belgrade) football club Crvena Zvezda [Red Star], orders a burek with *ajvar* (a red-pepper relish, sometimes referred to as "Serbian salsa"). And he's not joking. He of course has to repeat the order. His unusual order elicits amazement from his "Slovene" friends, Buddha and Storž:

> *Buddha: "With ajvar? How can you eat that? With ajvar, that's for the Finns."*
> *Ortič: "What Finns?"*
> *Storž: "You can't eat it with ajvar, you can eat hod dok [hot dog] with ajvar, but burek you eat with cheese."*
> *Ortič: "But I don't..." [in Serbo-Croatian]*
> *[Ortič is left speechless. A fourth friend, Turcin, probably the child of Bosnian parents, orders a pizza burek.]* [231]

231 Mitja Okorn, *Tu pa tam* [Here and There] (Dallas Records, 2004).

In a critique of the film in *Mladina* entitled "Ponarejeni čapci" [Knock-off Čapci] (čapci = members of the subculture of descendants of immigrants), the cast is summarized and interpreted as follows:

> *For instance Ortič ordering a burek with ajvar. In that tiny, naïve moment when the youth in a Red Star uniform repeats his order, you can see the unfamiliarity with the actual customs and tradition of that which he represents with his newly overdone street uniform of a generation of čapci, who did not go to Mostar on their secondary-school trip or serve in the Yugoslav National Army and spent their summer holidays with their relatives in the south in order to learn their culinary and cultural habits. The film presents a real generation which tends towards cultural imitation of an environment in which they actually do not want to live. But they are proud of their roots, and therefore they flaunt them. And they are aware of it.*[232]

Of course the cast could be explained and interpreted very differently. It could also be read as a kind of policy—if we can even use that expression in this case—of destruction of or in fact outmanoeuvring the existing nationalistic stereotypes. Therefore the things that are ascribed to southerners, at least in this film, are turned on their heads. They—southerners, Bosnians, čefurji—should already know that you don't eat burek with ajvar! This strategy could therefore also be understood as a kind of oppositional or alternative practice or mode of expression.

The outmanoeuvring of stereotypes could actually be found in numerous very different statements, or signifiers of practices. In the area of production for instance in the recipes for the "euroburek" (a pie with spinach, meat and cheese),[233] or for "a little more SLO and veggie, and mushrooms for a change," which hides beneath the telling title "So that the Burek won't be a Turek" ("Turk"—was and still is a pejorative

232 Tomica Šuljić, "Ponarejeni čapci" [Knock-off Čapci], *Mladina*, January 31, 2005, 59.
233 Šalehar, "Prvi Evrogrižljaj," 57.

expression for "*orientalci*," "easterners," i.e. foreigners from the east).[234] In the area of consumption for instance in the various (to a greater or lesser extent institutionalized) parties, shows, events, film premieres, and comic strips. The premiere of the above-mentioned low-budget feature film *Tu pa tam* at the Kolosej [Coliseum] movie complex in Ljubljana was followed by a "crazy burek party in Oz."[235] In response to the question "what did that look like?" the film's PR rep said: "yeah, [it was] no after party—people got together and ate bureks and drank yogurt." And to the question "Why a burek party?": "Because it's a traditional Slovenian dish[.]"[236] So stereotypes are sometimes outmanoeuvred by a combination of nutritional elements. At the opening party for the Slovene Advertising Festival in 2004, "everything [was] in the style of the film (*Kajmak in marmelada*), everything in a Bosnian/Slovene combination." They ate bureks and potica and drank yogurt and refošk (Slovenian refosco wine).[237] The second issue of *Stripburek*, subtitled "Comics from the other Europe," travelled to numerous exhibitions, comic and other festivals and events throughout Europe after its publication in 2001. At an independent exhibition in Paris they served meat and cheese bureks made by one of the authors of the publication.[238] And what do you think the author of this book served after the publication of his doctoral thesis on the burek in Slovenia? Carniolan sausage?[239]

But all of the above statements can also be read or understood as incorporation or inclusion. Yes, the very thing that we so vehemently stated in the preceding chapter, and then forgot about. That is, as the process through which the burek approaches or touches on the dominant pattern.

---

234 Šalehar, "Da burek ne bo Turek," 57.

235 K. R., "Tu pa tam drevi končno v kinu" [Here and There Finally Makes It to the Cinema], *Delo*, January 26, 2005, 9.

236 PR representative for the film *Tu pa tam*, e-mail message to author, September 27, 2005.

237 Maja Remi, "Plavolasi nizozemski kajmak" [Blond Dutch Kajmak], *Nedelo*, February 29, 2004, 17.

238 Katerina Mirović and Ivan Mitrevski, conversation, summer, 2005, and Katerina Mirović, telephone conversation, summer, 2006.

239 If he had been cool enough, he would have. I did serve Carniolan sausage to the members of the dissertation committee at my thesis defence, which among other things I dropped on the floor in order to demonstrate that the force of gravity operates on it uncompromisingly. The reason that I served Carniolan sausage and not bureks at my thesis defence was primarily practical: a burek if dropped to the floor would turn into an unappetizing mush.

We have said that incorporation or inclusion play out on two levels, via two processes: (a) through the conversion of alternative or oppositional signifiers—i.e. signifiers which stand in opposition to the dominant culture—into products of mass production, which Dick Hebdige called the commodity form; and (b) through the labelling and redefining by dominant groups of the practices, styles, behaviours and objects which the dominant culture finds disturbing so that they fit into their conceptual frameworks—which Hebdige calls the ideological form. In this process of ideological, conceptual inclusion, these non-conformist, disturbing to the dominant culture practices and objects can (b1) on one hand be trivialized, naturalized, domesticated—differentness thus being transformed into equality, the difference is denied; and (b2) on the other hand, as Hebdige shows, the differentness can be turned into a spectacle, a clown, a scandal—the difference is thus emphasized or exhibited.[240]

Both points and the subpoints can also be found in the life of the burek in Slovenia. Let's begin at the end for a change. Emphasizing the differences, a kind of burekfoolery, can also be seen in the majority of the above statements, from the "burek with ajvar" film cast in the film *Tu pa tam*[241] to the various parties, for instance the burek and potica, yogurt and refošk "in the style of the film" *Kajmak in marmelada* at the opening party for the Slovene Advertising Festival.[242]

The denial of differences, a kind of burekdomestication, can also be found in some of the above statements, for instance in the recipe for the "euroburek"[243] and in the recipe for "a little more SLO and veggie, and mushrooms for a change" burek.[244] But in order to avoid the fatal impression of hermeticism of the selected stories, let's look for a burekexample in a story about healthy lifestyles. Remember Saša Einsiedler's disclosure in *Nedelo* about taking a "classical recipe for burek and add[ing] her own touches."[245] And when the anonymous reporter from *Pilot* asked her what dish she would cook for him or her, she

240 Hebdige, *Subculture*, 97.
241 Okorn, *Tu pa tam*.
242 Remi, "Plavolasi nizozemski kajak," 17.
243 Šalehar, "Prvi Evrogrižljaj," 57.
244 Šalehar, "Da burek ne bo Turek," 57.
245 Klavdija, "Začinjena pita za mesojedce," 55.

again spoke only of cooking "meat pie à la Saša," which was a result of an attempt at burekmaking.[246] And since we have recalled Saša's burek, then it would only be right to remember Saška's burek, the story about how "everyone's favourite pop singer [...] swallow[ed] her sorrows after her (un)professional appearance at the EMAs [the Slovenian selection for the Eurovision Song Contest]."[247] The same event was reported in another publication under the headline "After the EMAs she went out for a burek," in which Saška Lendero sumptuously describes buying two boxes of bureks and the "burek party" that followed.[248] Of course, this article, published in *Nova* (a Slovenian tabloid), particularly in the context of its sensationalist headline, can be read as a kind of burekfoolery.

Inclusion therefore proves to be a kind of discursive alleviation, literarily speaking, as a sort of epic return to the unconditioned roots. So it can be understood it as a vanquishing of stereotyping, burekalization and other sinister processes. But on the other hand it can also be read as a mode of expression custom-made for Slovenes—for non-burek defined people—which does not threaten their world. Inclusion thus places the burek inside the dominant conceptual, semantic framework. To put it slightly differently, the attitude towards the burek is set in relation to "us," the majority.

In this science of power/knowledge, if we can speak of science at all, we are caught in a vicious cycle of continuous questioning and unclear, uncertain, ever-changing answers.

The metaburek therefore has to be understood, interpreted, and conceptualized not just as a complex of some discursive coherency, but also as a complex of mutual contradictoriness. And, as seems to be particularly important for us at this juncture, as a complex of inconclusiveness, which means that the metaburek does not allow unilateral and absolute conclusions.

The metaburek therefore has to be understood primarily or purely as a complex excess, which is already implicated in its name. An excess

---

246 Anon., "Imejmo se radi."

247 A. Z., "Saškin burek," 12.

248 Marjanca Likovič, "Po Emi odšla na burek" [After the EMAs She Went Out for a Burek], *Nova*, February 20, 2006, 40–41.

which can never be precisely defined. It is always there, but there is always something more.[249]

I have intentionally concluded this story about the symbolic life of the burek in Slovenia with some material facts or strategies. Intentional? Yes, intentional, so I could at least partially escape these fearsome discourses. But is this even possible? Let's ask this in a different way: is this commodity normalization—an explanation of which, if you recall, I promised at the end—at all possible to discuss separately from ideological normalization? Are they not closely intertwined, inseparable processes? But the question doesn't need an answer, does it? The burek thus has also physically swum its way into the Slovenian nutritional mainstream. By the end of the millennium they had begun to serve it in the Slovenian Army, you could find it in Slovenian schools, on some flights on Adria Airways, etc., etc. But this of course does not mean that doors everywhere were opened to the burek, much less wide open. Of course this thriving consumption could not occur without thriving production. Slovenian production, which now even produces bureks for the markets of the former SFRY, including burekcountry numero uno, Bosnia and Herzegovina.[250] So we are now exporting bureks to the very place from which we once imported them! Is history repeating itself or rolling over? Rolling over like a dead man in a grave when things are said, written and done in his name which he couldn't have imagined in his wildest dreams.

249 The author's original term for the metaburek was *burekov več*, which literally translates as "the burek's 'more'." This poetic construction unfortunately could not be rendered gracefully in English (t.n.).

250 With some help from the (Slovenian) Mercator supermarket chain.

Afterburek

The burek—Marx's words once again are right on target—"appears, at first sight, a very trivial thing, and easily understood. Its analysis shows that it is, in reality, a very queer thing, abounding in metaphysical subtleties and theological niceties." If the burek—still leaning on Marx—is the unconditioned burek, "there is nothing mysterious about it [...] but, so soon as it steps forth as [the metaburek], it is changed into something transcendent." It no longer feeds merely hungry stomachs, but it stands on its head before all other bureks, and evolves out of its greasy brain grotesque ideas, far more wonderful than it would ever have chomped from itself.[1]

In the analysis of the metaburek, these substantive, semantic, and power-relation multi-complexities, these transcendent things, a very hybrid methodology or, better, perspective was applied. Undoubtedly there will be some whiner, some scientific nit-picker, who will maintain that it isn't a methodology at all. But let's leave the whiners, nit-pickers and the rest of the scientific inventory aside for a moment. I employed very different approaches, looked into several areas and juxtaposed them—without respect for great things, imperiously flaunting

1 Marx, as we know, is speaking about commodities. About commodities as *use value* and about commodities which appear *as commodities*. The analogy with the unconditioned burek and the metaburek is thus not completely unreasonable: "So far as it is a value in use, there is nothing mysterious about it [...]. But, so soon as it steps forth *as a commodity*, it is changed into something transcendent. It not only stands with its feet on the ground, but, in relation to all other commodities, it stands on its head, and evolves out of its wooden brain grotesque ideas, far more wonderful than table-turning ever was." (Marx, *Capital*, 81) Marx is of course referring to spiritual séances, which achieved exceptional popularity during the second half of the 19th century, a time of great trust in science (see Mladen Dolar, *Prozopopeja* [Prosopopoeia] [Ljubljana: Analecta, 2006], 74).

their various authorities, references and other garbage—widely differing and often incompatible things. For instance, serious science and idiotic jokes. How audacious, how cheeky, how suicidal, right?

But despite the sizeable and widely varying range of statements included in the analysis, this text is still far from a general overview of the metaburek. I am well aware of these deficiencies. Cooking up dishes as complex as the metaburek will continue and persist due to its richness. All I have done, to recycle Said's metaphor, is to describe the parts of this dish and merely to suggest the existence of a larger whole, detailed, interesting, dotted with fascinating figures, events, places, objects, situations and more.[2]

This burekwork thus has not brought verifiable and eternal rules or recipes. It is strategic, eclectic, adapted to the nature of the observed object. An observed object that knows no easy peace, which changes constantly, which continuously regenerates, perhaps is even born anew. But rather than the genesis, let's focus here on the ontology of the metaburek.

Despite its continuously changing nature, the metaburek is internally consistent. It is not just a light, carefree game; it has an articulated—sometimes even extremely well articulated—series of relationships with the culture around it. And that has also been the essence, the central question, or if you will, the hypothesis of my work. To capture, understand, gain insight into at least a piece of this consistence, this articulated string of the embeddedness, or better interwovenness, of the metaburek in the culture around it.

I hope that I have at least indicated or suggested that it is not a case of simple mechanical translation of great facts, discourses, self-evidence, knowledge, and truths onto such a complex matter as the metaburek. There are nationalistic and antinationalistic metabureks, there are scientific and fictional metabureks, there are dominant and oppositional metabureks, etc. But these relations of the nationalistic metaburek include a series of momentums, factors and circumstances which

2 Said, *Orientalism*, 24.

in the end are clearly reflected in the complexity, diversity and uniqueness of nationalistic burekstatements or the nationalistic metaburek itself, if we can in fact even speak so self-evidently and authoritatively. In other words, these nationalistic or any other form of burekstatements are not exactly a homogenous and compact entity; they can be approached only through various alienated research or academic perspectives, because the making of nationalistic burekstatements touches on numerous widely different areas, includes different strategies and techniques, represents various interests and kinds of knowledge, etc. It is therefore necessary to research each example or statement separately in order to figure out whom to thank for its existence. Did particular needs and local conditions come to the surface, or were there some larger power/knowledge strategies at work?

In my analysis of the metaburek I paid more attention to those larger strategies, entities, those... discourses. I tried to understand—and in no way am I saying that I did so conscientiously and well—these discursive entities, for instance the nationalistic metaburek, as a complex game of supports and mutual, complex obligations of various mechanisms of signification and power, and not (just) as self-evident products of one or another form of homogenization (such as e.g. national discourse).

It seems important to point out, and to do so at the top of my lungs, that through my efforts one will not get an analysis of discourses, but an analysis of an object which is subject to discourses. It is therefore a shift of focus from an analysis of discourses to an analysis of a discursive object. It is not a discovery of some kind of rules of discursive rules, modes, their inner workings and other things which transformed the object. It is an understanding of the (discursive) transformation of the object itself. This difference might seem paltry, unimportant, merely stylistic, but it is Cyclopic at least on one point. That is, this kind of analytic gambit requires that we also analyze the broader, non-discursive, extra-discursive context which is at work in the formation of the meta-burek. And not just that. It also or even primarily requires that we analyze or at least understand the object itself, the object in its unconditionality, its extra-discursivity. Only in this way can we understand this complex transformation from the realm of a material, physical belly-filler to the realm of culture, signification, power, this "crime against the natural order." In no way do I want my project to appear to be an attempt to extract evidentness from the primary material unity, to show it as a quasi-evidentness, to proclaim that there is no solid point from which other questions could be posed.

And what in fact is happening to the object under these fearsome forces of discourse? (a) Materially, substantively speaking, discourses first of all dematerialize the object. Actually it is a rematerialization; they carry it to some other order of materiality. They create out of the nutritional burek a written, spoken, photographed, represented burek. Out of food they make sound, written text, spoken words, photographs, internet jokes. But discourses also change, and modify, its primary, nutritional materiality, although in a different, more insidious manner. They make it less greasy, smaller, made with Slovenian curds or in the form of large capital letters: ART.[3]

And now we are very close to point (b). Discourses furthermore carry the burek out of the realm of unconditionality, innocence and purity into the field of signification, meanings and knowledge. This, undoubtedly a crucial enterprise for the burek, transforms it from a belly-filler into culture. Semiotically speaking, the burek, i.e. food, the material world, is brought into the realm of text. It is made greasy, Balkan, Slovene, not-Slovene, the greatest, eastern, awesome, crap, Oriental, unhealthy, traditional, plebeian, čefurski, A.B.S., junk, a cherub. In listing this conceptual diversity we might give some serious consideration to its above all violent reduction into two stories, two conceptual categories. A profound violence done to the metaburek, a huge, perhaps the greatest sin in the book, for which, I'm afraid, no well-considered word, no well-conceived apology will suffice.

Of course alongside this conceptual diversity it is necessary to underscore the long, complex and intricate genesis of the metaburek. A painstaking semantic improvement, amendment and perfecting. All of these numerous burekmeanings didn't happen overnight, didn't appear by God's or some other decree, didn't fall from the sky (like a Coke

3 Borut Peterlin, photo, in Anon., "Piera Ravnikar, programska direktorica" [Piera Ravnikar, Program Director], *Mladina*, September 16, 2006, p. 63.

bottle in the Kalahari). But what a twisted path, dotted with interesting events, and various metamorphoses, the metaburek has taken to arrive from the unconditioned burek to the above-cited statement: "I admit that I love Jurek more than burek. Anyone who thinks Jurek is a burek, is a burek."[4] Meanings thus never have boring histories, geneses, development. And that history is never (merely) a coincidental, idealistic history, but (also) a materialistic history, a history of material realities, material limitations, material differences. A history of material differences? Well, perhaps in this concluding chapter I should not stray too far from the text. Therefore let's say a history of those that have the power to signify, and those that don't.

And now we unavoidably find ourselves at point (c), which has actually imposed itself on us since the very beginning of the last point. When the burek is brought into the realm of culture, into the field of signification, it is at the same time, without any real possibility of escape, also thrown into the realm of politics. The burek thus becomes invested with power, becomes interwoven, crisscrossed with battles for meaning, self-evidence, knowledge, truth. It is celebrated, repudiated, not mentioned, sanctioned, changed, stigmatized, glorified, included, jokes are made about it. But these jokes rarely if ever occur in a vacuum—a place not created by the vectors of power. The burek is therefore not (just) an object in a carefree game of signification, but is deeply entrenched in the political realm. In other words, cultural products cannot be understood without understanding the power relations within which they are produced. Culture is not, at least we are told by the example of the metaburek, a space of homogenous power, but a space of numerous complex battles, conflicts, debates, strange unexpected alliances and coalitions, and much else that has a whiff of power. The burek's inescapability from power relations, the entrenching of the burek in the political realm, is finally demonstrated by the spectre of various authorities, fields, institutions, disciplines, "dictatorships" which are in one way or another invested in this apparently trivial, marginal, negligible object. But in contemplating the burek's multi-complexity

4 Buldožer, "Biatlonci na priprave v zmrzovalnik" [Biathletes Training in a Freezer], *Večer*, February 17, 1999, 42.

with respect to power we must confess to a further sin: a violent reduction to some forms of dominant and on the other side alternative and/or oppositional discourses, or to rejecting and excluding and on the other side approving and affirmative approaches, phenomena, procedures and discourses. As we stated above, the metaburek is the product of a complex game of supports and mutual obligations of various mechanisms of power, and not (just) some larger power strategies. In other words, the metaburek reflects not only big, obvious power relations, but also conceals numerous particular, miniature relations, which are woven into these patterns of power in very complex ways. Teasing them out, believe me, is no simple task.

In pursuing this unsimple task, I have avoided what Foucault calls "labyrinthine questions", such as: "Who then has power and what has he in mind?"[5] Since this is not a study of power or a study of the outward appearance of power, but more of a story of the outward appearance of power in relation to its victims, its application, the object to which it attaches itself and produces its real effects. It is therefore an analysis of how the phenomena, techniques and procedures of power enter into the game on the most basic level. Thus an analysis of victims and not power. In other words, instead of seeking the sovereign in its exalted isolation I have focused my research on the other end entirely. I am therefore attempting to discover how this complex object, the metaburek, is gradually constituted through the multitudes of forces, energies, desires and thoughts related to power.

So! The burek, through a process of transformation of phenomena, is reborn as the metaburek, a complex social and cultural object. And this object is not, as we have now said many times, some kind of alienated consciousness, an illusion or an ideology, but a real, living, developing thing. It is not a construct, as is often so facilely and mechanically said these days in social science, but a living, material, either fragrant or stinking reality. Do you dare call a low-fat cheese burek with 6.4 grams of fat an illusion, an alienated consciousness, a construct?

---

5 Foucault, *History of Sexuality*, 97.

This should be enough for the Afterburek, a chapter in which, as the unwritten rule says, nothing new or unknown should be written, but everything should merely be summarized, resolved, concluded. This point—a point of contact with scientific self-evidence and hidden scientific discipline—also seems an appropriate place to say a word or two about the types of knowledge which accompany this text (and which in the final analysis in fact formed the metaburek). So something about science! Do you still remember the questions from the beginning of the book? I should repeat them, so you won't have to bother turning the pages: can my purportedly scientific field—the interpretation of these human affairs—be anything other than non-scientific, i.e. everyday interpretive human behaviour, other than my subject itself and humanities research in general? But you will get no answer from me. That, I'm afraid, could cost me my head. Only the realization—a kind of roundabout answer—that I have come to through this scientific effort: science—and here I do not mean only social science—should not be considered an infallible arbiter with regard to truth and reality. Just think how boring it would be to live only with healthy bureks, or without any bureks whatsoever. Paul Feyerabend begins his book by saying: "Science is an essentially anarchistic enterprise."[6] Here this sounds merely entertaining. But when it is about life and death, when the blood begins to flow, whose side will you be fighting on? And again a roundabout answer: I'll be for the burek.

6 Feyerabend, *Against Method*, 17.

Burekbibliography

PRIMARY SOURCES

List of burekstatements cited and other statements to a greater or lesser extent connected with bureks

The burekstatements are intentionally not separated or divided into separate sections (e.g. periodicals, websites, conversations, e-mail message to authors, etc.). Such a division would emphasize that there are significant, perhaps even insurmountable differences between them. Of course the statements are very different, in terms of materiality, place of occurrence, and with it spatial range, lifetime or better chronological range, capacity to produce effects, etc. But at the same time, all of the statements were written about a specific object. Thus: burekstatements![1]

---

1 In entering the statements in the archive I encountered various technical difficulties, which frequently, if not always, arose from conceptual and theoretical dilemmas. I will list only a few, both the difficulties and the solutions.
When citing websites I entered the date on which I last visited the website. Websites experience significantly more existential uncertainty than print materials. Don't be too sure that you will still be able to find the statements on the website cited or that the page or the website still exists.
Many of the statements are original statements in periodicals, which I found in online or electronic archives of the newspapers and in the magazines. The date in this case is the date of publication of the periodical, which can be very misleading, since they were often published later on the web. I didn't want to load the text down with a lot of question marks. Question marks which, not necessarily in physical form, are already very often hanging in the text, thrust deep into the soft, warm, greasy burekmeat. But if we take them in our hands in order to bite into the delicious burek—perhaps even hoping that with their help we won't get our hands greasy—they turn out to be unwieldy, awkward, or superfluous. I therefore finish the text—as is most fitting for such a serious scientific tome—with an exclamation.

Ales6m. http://www.kulinarika.net/recept.asp?ID=3337 (March 23, 2015).
Ali En. "Sirni & mesni. In: *Leva scena*, Ali En. Prodok—mačji disk, 1994.
Anon. http://web.s-gim.kr.edus.si/projekti/timko/2001_2002/burekteam/hpbbr/burek.htm (visited August 2, 2007).
Anon. http://www.drustvo-gurman.si/recipes.php?S=6&Article=699 (August 2, 2007).
Anon. http://web.s-gim.kr.edus.si/projekti/timko/2001_2002/burekteam/hpbbr/recepti.htm (August 2, 2007).
Anon. http://razvezanijezik.org/?page=burek (March 23, 2015).
Anon. "Anti Burek Sistem (A. B. S.)." Name of project of Slovene skinhead group SLOI.
Anon. "Burek." In *Slovar slovenskega knjižnega jezika. Prva knjiga* [Dictionary of Slovenian Literary Language: First Volume], edited by Anton Bajec, Ivanka Kozlevčar, France novak, Korošec Tomo, and Ada Vidovič Muha, 226. Ljubljana: DZS, 1970.
Anon. "Burek bi džamije pa ne, a?" Ljubljana grafito.
Anon. "Burek? nein danke." Ljubljana grafito.
Anon. "Burek si" [You're a burek]. Phraseme in Slovene slang.
Anon. "Burekmajstri" [Burekmasters]. Nickname for Albanians and partially for other immigrants from the former republics of the SFRY.
Anon. Caption to Blaž Samec's photo. *Delo*, July 12, 2005, 9.
Anon. "Doći ćemo po ono struju i sendviče!!!" [We're Coming for Electricity and Sandwiches!!!]. *Večer*, January 12, 1999, 41.
Anon. "Evrobalkan." Name of fast-food chain.
Anon. Photomontage. In Berto Ritotreb, "Mladinamit." *Mladina*, January 12, 2004, 72.
Anon. Photomontage. In Tropinovec, "Slovenska kokoška je ogrožena" [The Slovenian Hen is Endangered], *Večer*, December 16, 2004, 41.
Anon. "Gostinsko podjetje Ljubljana, Ljubljana, Streliška ulica 12, vabi k sodelovanju" [Ljubljana Food Service Company, Ljubljana, Streliška Street 12, Invitation to Participate]. *Večer*, November 19, 1971, 6.
Anon. "Imejmo se radi" [Let's Love Each Other]. *Pilot*, March 27, 2005.
Anon. "Izgledaš kot burek" [You look like a burek]. Phraseme in Slovene slang.
Anon. "Izjave tedna" [Quotes of the Week]. *Slovenske novice*, February 1, 2006, 12.
Anon. "Jutri na mizi" [On the Table Tomorrow]. *Večer*, March 6, 1963, 4.
Anon. "Katarina Čas. Ljubiteljica bureka in vampov" [Katarina Čas. Lover of Bureks and Tripe]. *Nova*, March 19, 2007, 49.
Anon. Image. In Anon., "Manipulator." *Mladina*, December 15, 1989, 12.
Anon. "Nimaš za burek." Phraseme in Slovene slang.
Anon. "Novomeška kronika" [Novo Mesto Chronicle]. *Dolenjski list*, September 22, 1966, 13.
Anon. "Rolanje po sceni" [Roller-skating through the Scene]. *Mladina*, January 14, 1992, 11.
Anon. "Recepti Janeza Štruklja" [The Recipes of Janez Štrukelj]. *Večer*, August 9, 2001, 34.
Anon. "Proglas priseljevanje" [The Immigration Manifesto]. *Mladina*, January 23, 2006, 1.
Anon. Untitled. *Večer*, July 29, 1998, 42.
Anon. "Volimo Jureka više od bureka." Word play, widespread in Slovene and in certain other languages of the former SFRY.
Anon. "Znaki, da ste odrasli ..." [Signs that You're an Adult...]. *Večer*, July 11, 2002, 36.
A. Z. "Saškin burek" [Saška's Burek]. *Slovenske novice*, February 1, 2006, 12.
Baš, Angelos, ed. *Slovenski etnološki leksikon* [Slovenian Ethnological Dictionary]. Ljubljana, Mladinska knjiga, 2004.
Bašin, Igor. Conversation, June 7, 2005.
Bašin, Igor. Telephone conversation, March 24, 2006.

Berishaj, Martin. Conversation, May 20, 2005.
Berk, Ksenija. Telephone conversation, February 23, 2005.
Bgajo. http://www.kulinarika.net/recept.asp?ID=4599 (March 23, 2015).
Bogataj, Janez. E-mail message to author, April 11, 2007.
Bogataj, Janez. E-mail message to author, April 12, 2007.
Borko, Manca. "Za Plečnika jim ni mar" [They Don't Give a Damn about Plečnik]. *Delo*, December 2, 2004, 6.
bosna_majka.http://obala.net/index.php?show=news&action=news&id=9925&comments_perpage=13&comments_pa (June 7, 2005)
B. P. "Vsak dan sveži burek v Mariboru" [Fresh Bureks Every Day in Maribor]. *Večer*, May 29, 1965, 4.
B. P. "Prizrenski Burek iz Slovenske ulice" [Prizren Bureks from a Slovenian Street]. *Večer*, May 18, 1966, 4.
Buldožer. "Biatlonci na priprave v zmrovalnik" [Biathletes Training in a Freezer]. *Večer*, February 17, 1999, 42.
Crnkovič, Marko. "Burek za Jelinčiča" [A Burek for Jelinčič]. *Naši razgledi*, August 14, 1992, 477.
Cuder, Tomaž. "Pred izbrisom" [Before Deletion]. *Večer, Sobotna priloga*, April 23, 2005, 34.
Čakarić, Maja. "Na šolsko kosilo pridejo le učitelji" [Only Teachers Eat the School Lunch]. *Delo*, January 13, 2006, 6.
Čakš, Aleš. "Prva želja – hamburger" [First Choice – Hamburger]. *Delo*, March 21, 2001, 3.
Čančula, Miha. E-mail message to author, July 2006 ,13.
Čančula, Miha. E-mail message to author, July 2006 ,12.
Čančula, Miha. http://www.geocities.com/metalec_mobitela/fore/BMashina.doc (August 2007 ,27).
Černe, Tea. "Le kaj bi Slovenci brez bureka in baklave?" [What Would Slovenians Be without Bureks and Baklava?]. *Nedelo*, November 9, 2003, 24.
Čibej, Boris. E-mail message to author, April 2005 ,2.
Čop, Kajetan and Alice Čop. "Burek teater." Name of acting group.
Dalaj Eegol. E-mail message to author, July 13, 2005.
Dalaj Eegol. E-mail message to author, July 16, 2005.
Dalaj Eegol. E-mail message to author, May 27, 2006.
Davenport, Fionn. *Best of Ljubljana: The Ultimate Pocket Guide & Map*. Footscray, Oakland, London: Lonely Planet Publications, 2006.
Dežurni reporter. "Sir" [Cheese]. *Večer*, June 23, 1967, 2.
Director of the Orehek bakery. Telephone conversation, June 2006.
Djurić, Branko. *Kajmak in marmelada* [Cheese and Jam]. ATA Productions, 2003.
D. M. "Prve izkušnje samopostrežne restavracije v Mariboru" [First Impressions of a Self-Service Restaurant in Maribor]. *Večer*, November 10, 1962, 4.
Drobnič, Janez. http://www.dz-rs.si/index.php?id=97&cs=1&mandate
=3&unid=SZA3%7C0BB452F81225B7ACC1256EBB0030795F&s
howdoc=1 (August 27, 2007).
Dugorepec, Toni. Photo. In Jure Aleksič, "Rdeči November" [Red November], *Mladina*, November 23, 2007, 46.
Editorial board of *Stripburger*. *Stripburek*, name of thematic issue of *Stripburger*.
Forbici, Goran. Conversation, winter 2007.
Fornezzi, Tone. "Volimo Jureka više od bureka!" [We Love Jurek More than Burek!]. *Nedeljski dnevnik*, February 26, 2006, 14.

Gazdič Sašo. E-mail message to author, April 20, 2008.

Grafenauer, Stanko. *Kuhinja naše družine* [Our Family Cuisine]. Ljubljana: Mladinska knjiga, 2002.

Gregorčič, Marta. "Vikingi ali Valhala – skinheadi Slovenije" [Vikings or Valhalla – Skinheads of Slovenia]. In *Urbana plemena. Subkulture v Sloveniji v devetdesetih* [Urban Tribes: Subcultures in Slovenia in the Nineties] edited by Peter Stankovič, Gregor Tomc, and Mitja Velikonja, 97–110. Ljubljana: Študentska založba, 1999.

Grom, Staša. http://www.maxximum-portal.com/sport/313.html (July 12, 2006).

Gruden, Mateja. "Domača kuhinja je najboljša učiteljica." *Delo*, October 23, 2001, 9.

Gruden, Mateja. "Vse je (bilo) narobe, nihče ni ukrepal" [Everything Is (Was) Wrong, [but] Nobody Did Anything about It]. *Delo*, December 11, 2003, 7.

Grunf. http://www.kulinarika.net/recept.asp?ID=10675 (March 23, 2015).

Guzelj, Igor. "Se še znamo zabavati?" [Do We Still Know How to Have Fun?]. *Teleks*, August 1, 1980, 27.

Hladnik-Milharčič, Ervin. "Šunka v evru, 25 kuharjev, 60 natakarjev 80 jedi in 1350 gostov" [Ham Shaped like a Euro, 25 Cooks, 60 Waiters, 80 Dishes and 1350 Guests]. *Dnevnik, Objektiv*, January 20, 2007, 16–18.

Hočevar, Meta. "Smoletov vrt" [Smole's Orchard]. In *Smoletov vrt: komedija v treh dejanjih* [Smole's Orchard: Three Acts Comedy], edited by Meta Hočevar, 37–60. Ljubljana: SNG Ljubljana, 2006.

Hojs, Ana. "Energijska gostota hitre hrane" [The Energy Density of Fast Food]. *Zdravstveno varstvo* 37 (1998): 47–50.

Ivanc, Jera. "Slovenija, odkod lepote tvoje ..." [Slovenia, From Whence Comes Your Beauty ...]. In *Smoletov vrt: komedija v treh dejanjih* [Smole's Orchard: Three Acts Comedy], edited by Meta Hočevar, 7–10. Ljubljana: SNG Ljubljana, 2006. Three Acts Comedy.

Jesenko, Anže. E-mail message to author, March 21, 2005.

Jesenko, Anže. E-mail message to author, March 22, 2005.

Jesenko, Anže. http://burek.uni.cc (August 16, 2006).

Jež, Boris. "Razglednica iz Ljubljane" [Postcard from Ljubljana]. *Delo, Sobotna priloga*, September 18, 1999, 44.

Jež, Boris. "Bo Martin Strel naša blagovna znamka" [Will Martin Strel Be Our National Trademark?]. *Delo, Sobotna priloga*, July 3, 2004, 23.

Jež, Boris. "Galerija, črpalka, trgovina ... Smo se za to borili?" [A Gallery, a Gas Station, a Shop... Is This What We Were Fighting For?]. *Delo, Sobotna priloga*, June 19, 2004, 13.

Jež, Boris. "Diktatura kranjske klobase" [The Dictatorship of the Carniolan Sausage]. *Delo, Sobotna priloga*, February 28, 2004, 4.

Jež, Boris. "Zanimiv košček nebes" [An Interesting Slice of Heaven]. *Delo, Sobotna priloga*, July 15, 2006, 13.

Jež, Dušan. *Grafiti Ljubljane* [The Graffiti of Ljubljana]. Ljubljana: Noviforum, 2005.

Josipovič, Damir. Telephone conversation, April 2, 2007.

Jukič, Boris. Three-frame comic strip. *Delo*, July 18, 2005, 8.

-k. "Burek iz gabrske pekarne" [Bureks from the Gaberska Bakery]. *Večer*, September 11, 1980, 6.

Kermauner, Aksinja. *Dnevnik Hiacinte Novak. V znamenju Tehtnice.* Miš, Dob pri Domžalah, 2003.

Knez, Primož. "Do bureka le s papirji" [You Need to Have Papers for a Burek]. *Dnevnik*, November 16, 1999, 17.

Klavdija, Miko. "Začinjena pita za mesojedce" [Savory Pie for Meat-Eaters]. *Ona*, February 3, 2004, 55.

Klemenčič, Jakob, and Marcel Ruijters. Illustration. In *Stripburek: Comics from Behind the Rusty Iron Curtain*, edited by Katerina Mirović, back cover. Ljubljana: Forum Ljubljana – Stripburger, 1997.

Klinar, Aleš, and Urban Centa. "Jasmina." In *Agropop, Pesmi s Triglava*. ZKP RTV Slovenija, 1986.

Kojič, Tili. "Mojstru za njoke dišijo tartufi" [Smell of Truffles Delights Gnocchi Master]. *Viva*, January, 2003, 92.

K. R. "Tu pa tam drevi končno v kinu" [Here and There Finally Makes It to the Cinema]. *Delo*, January 26, 2005, 9.

Krstić, Goran. conversation, fall 2006.

Krstić, Goran. e-mail message to author. April 30, 2007.

Kršić, Dejan. "Burek." In *Leksikon Yu mitologije* [Lexicon of Yugoslavian Mythology], edited by Đorđe Matić, Vladimir Arsenijević, and Iris Andrić, 65. Zagreb, Belgrade: Rende, Postscriptum, 2004.

"Kulinarična Slovenija." http://www.kulinarika.net/baze/receptirezultati.
asp?besede=burek (March 23, 2015).

Kunarac, Milojka. Conversation, summer 2006.

Kurtović, Aida. Conversation, June 2005.

Kuzmin, Bruno. "Zjutraj nimaš za burek, zvečer je v žepu 30.000 dolarjev" [In the Morning Not Enough for a Burek, in the Evening 30,000 Dollars in Your Pocket]. *Delo*, June 7, 2003, 17.

Kužet, Zora. "'Moški vikend' v Ljubljani" ['Men's Weekend' in Ljubljana]. *Večer*, October 5, 2005, 35.

Owner of Dino Burek. telephone conversation, June 7, 2006.

Leteči. "Prvi spodad z burekom" [First Encounter with the Burek]. *Večer*, December 13, 1958, 3.

Likovič, Marjanca. "Po Emi odšla na burek" [After the EMAs She Went Out for a Burek]. *Nova*, February 20, 2006, 40–41.

Mal, Domen. "Obleka naredi vojaka" [The Clothes Make the Soldier]. *Več*, February 6, 2004, 24.

Marinka. http://www.kulinarika.net/recept.asp?ID=105 (March 23, 2015).

Marušič. Franc. http://www.delo.si/blog/ivanmars/index.php?BLOG_
PATH=220&BLOG_ARCHIVE (jesen 2006).

Medved, Meta, Kelšin, Nevenka, Miloševič, Nataša, Ulčakar, Tadej, and Primož Kus. "Prehrambene navade ljubljanskih osmošolcev" [Eating Habits among Primary School Children in Ljubljana]. *Zdravstveno varstvo* 37 (1998): 211–217.

Mehle, Borut. "Ena, ena, tri—burek ob pol noči" [One, One, Three, Burek at Midnight]. *Dnevnik*, December 23, 1999, 16.

Merc, Dušan. "Sit sem vseh teh tujcev" [I'm Sick of All these Foreigners]. *Večer, Sobotna priloga*, January 20, 2001, 33.

Meršnik, Manfred. "Zgrešeno mnenje, da nimamo kadrov" [The Erroneous Opinion that We Lack the Human Resources]. *Večer*, September 15, 2004, 33.

Mihelič, Primož. Conversation, July 2005.

Mirović, Katerina, and Ivan Mitrevski. Conversation, summer 2005.

Mirović, Katerina. Telephone conversation, summer 2006.

Mitrevski, Ivan. Conversation, summer 2005.

Mlekuž, Jernej. Serving bureks upon first defense of doctoral thesis, fall 2005.

Mlekuž, Jernej. "Slovenci z burekom v Evropo in/ali diktatura kranjske klobase: Nekaj o bureku, reprezentacijah bureka in 'slovenskem' etnonacionalnem diskurzu" [Slovenes into Europe with Bureks and/or the Dictatorship of the Carniolan Sausage: Some Thoughts on the Burek, Representations of the Burek and 'Slovene' Ethnonational Discourse]. *Dve domovini/Two Homelands* 23 (2006): 159–179.

Mlekuž, Jernej. "Predmet kot akter? Primer bureka v Sloveniji" [Object as Actor? The Case of the Burek in Slovenia]. PhD diss., University of Nova Gorica, 2008.

Mlinarič, Urška. "Post in obilo dobrot ob ramadanu" [Fasting and Abundance during Ramadan]. *Večer*, November 29, 2002, 14.

M. M. "Poznajo gostinsko abecedo" [They Know Their Restaurant ABCs]. *Večer*, October 23, 1963, 2.

Mrak, Marko. E-mail message to author, June 16, 2005.

Mrlješ, Radojko, Katičić; Jelena, Bogdanić-Đurić, Suzana, and Slobodan Jović. *Kuhinje Balkana: Razkošje okusov za vse priložnosti* [Cuisines of the Balkans: Luxury of Tastes for all Occasions]. Tržič: Učila International, 2005.

Nardin, Aleksander. "Zgodovina se ponavlja" [History is Repeating Itself]. *Delo*, May 6, 2004, 5.

Niet. http://www.sloport.net/forum/viewthread.php?tid=5920&page=5#neprebrano (September 15, 2006).

nm. "Kako ljubi Bosanec" [How a Bosnian Loves]. *Hopla*, November 21, 2003, 55.

n. n. "Praznik" [Holiday]. *Dnevnik*, September 2, 2004, 32.

Novak, Simon. "Mesto, ki je ohranilo dušo" [The Town which Kept Its Soul]. *Delo*, August 10, 2005, 17.

Okorn, Mitja. *Tu pa tam* [Here and There]. Dallas Records, 2004.

Pal, Nejc. "Mesni ali sirni? Sirni" [Meat or Cheese? Cheese]. *Večer*, March 4, 2005, 13.

Peterlin, Borut. Photo. In Anon., "Piera Ravnikar, programska direktorica" [Piera Ravnikar, Program Director]. *Mladina*, September 16, 2006, 63.

Pjević, J. "'Prosvijećeni' Štih" ['The Enlightened' Štih]. *Borba*, July 6, 1992.

Podjed, Dan. Telephone conversation, February 22, 2007.

Podkrižnik, Mimi. "Kakšno hrano jedo otroci v šoli?" [What Kind of Food Do Our Children Eat in School?]. *Delo*, April 18, 2000, 10.

Pokorn, Dražigost. telephone conversation, May 30, 2006.

Prajnić, Sandra. http://www.student-info.net/portal/portal.php?stran=
prva&vs=novice&id=173 (July 13, 2006).

Praprotnik, Nejc. "Jurij Schollmayer." *Večer*, November 19, 2004, 32.

PR representative for the film *Tu pa tam*. E-mail message to author, September 27, 2005.

Pušenjak, Dejan. "Desant na kajmak" [Landing in Kajmak]. *Večer*, August 12, 1991, 8.

Remec, Miha. *Mana. Časovni zapiski časnikarja Jurija Jereba* [Manna: Time Notes of Journalist Jurij Jereb]. Ljubljana: Tehniška založba Slovenije, 1985.

Remi, Maja. "Plavolasi nizozemski kajmak" [Blond Dutch Kajmak]. *Nedelo*, February 29, 2004, 17.

Repovž, Grega. "Tekma poceni denarja" [A Race for Easy Money]. *Delo, Sobotna priloga*, March 31, 2001, 8.

Ristović Čar, Ana. "Slovenščina za začetnike (situacijski slovar)" [Slovene for Beginners (A Situational Dictionary)]. *Delo, Sobotna priloga*, September 20, 2003, 14.

Samec, Blaž. Photo. *Delo*, July 12, 2005, 9.

Smasek, Lojze. "Posmehljivka v nadaljevanjih" [A Comedy in Several Acts]. *Večer*, June 12, 1992, 6.

Smerkolj, Primož. E-mail message to author, May 25, 2005.

Smerkolj, Primož. E-mail message to author, March 7, 2007.

Stankovič, Peter. "Rokerji s konca tisočletja." In *Urbana plemena. Subkulture v Sloveniji v*

devetdesetih, ed. Peter Stankovič, Gregor Tomc, Mitja Velikonja, Študentska založba, Ljubljana, 1999, 43–52.
Stankovič, Peter. "Burek? Ja, bitte!" *Dnevnik, Zelena pika*, January 15, 2005, 36–37.
Stankovič, Peter. http://www.fdv-kulturologija.si/kulturologija_kolumna.htm#Burek (spring 2007).
Stepišnik, Matija. "Od Jureta do bureka in druge zgodbe" [From Jure to Burek and Other Stories]. *Večer*, November 25, 2002, 5.
Stojič, Aljoša. "Oblak je faca" [Oblak is Cool]. *Večer*, September 23, 1999, 19.
Stojko Falk. Simon. Conversation, summer 2005.
Šabotić, Amra. Conversation, summer 2006.
Šabotić, Amra. Conversation, spring 2007.
Šajn, Gorazd. "Še dobro, da se povsod dobi burek" [Thank Goodness You Can Get a Burek Anywhere]. *Dnevnik*, July 23, 2003, 24.
Šalehar, Matevž. "Da burek ne bo Turek" [So that the Burek Won't Be a Turk]. *Večer*, January 23, 2004, 57.
Šalehar, Matevž. "Prvi Evrogrižljaj" [First Eurobite]. *Večer*, May 7, 2004, 57.
Šoštarič, Marjeta. "Slovenci z burekom v Evropo" [Slovenes into Europe with Bureks]. *Delo*, October 17, 2003, 4.
Šuljić, Tomica. "Ponarejeni čapci" [Knock-off Čapci]. *Mladina*, January 31, 2005, 59.
Šutej Adamič, Jelka, "Meso, žganje in divja etno glasba" [Meat, Spirits and Wild Ethno Music]. *Delo, Sobotna priloga*, February 27, 1999, 40.
Štajduhar, Meri. "Ćevap nacionalističkog okusa" [Ćevap with a Nationalist Flavour]. *Danas*, August 10, 1982, 48–49.
Štefančič, Marcel jr. "Kajmak in marmelada" [Cheese and Jam]. *Mladina*, November 17, 2003, 74.
Štih, Bojan. "To ni nobena pesem, to je ena sam ljubezen" [That's No Poem, That's Just Love]. *Naši razgledi*, June 11, 1982, 328–301.
Tamara. http://www.lunin.net/forum/index.php?showtopic=1358&hl=burek (March 23, 2015).
Technician at Pekarna Pečjak. Telephone conversation, June 19, 2006.
Technician at Žito. Telephone conversation, July 5, 2006.
Tivadar, Blanka. E-mail message to author, July 4, 2006.
Tomc, Gregor. E-mail message to author, March 16, 2005.
Vogrinc, Jure. Conversation, July 7, 2006.
Vogrinc, Jože. Written comments to author's doctoral thesis, June 2007.
Vranješ, Gajo. Telephone conversation, summer 2006.
Vulić, Gordana. "Mesni burek v prehrani, analiza kvalitete in predlog za izboljšanje" [The Meat Burek in Nutrition, an Analysis of Quality and Proposal for Improvement]. BA diss., University of Ljubljana, 1991.
Zajec, Diana. "Krotilci tigrov v šolskih klopeh" [Tiger Tamers on the School Benches]. *Delo*, September 4, 2000, 3.
Employees of Mladost snack bar. Telephone conversation, June 2006.
Zygo. http://www.gil-galad.info/smf/index.php?topic=213.0 (August 2, 2007).
Žerdin, Ali. E-mail message to author, March 2005 ,31.
Žerjavič, Peter. "Lov na tujce in geje" [Hunting for Foreigners and Gays]. *Delo*, December 31, 2003, 24.

LITERATURE

Althusser, Louis. "Ideology and Ideological State Apparatuses." In *Lenin and Philosophy and Other Essays*. Translated by Ben Brewster, 127–188. London: New Left Books, 1971.

Aristotele. *The Nicomachean Ethics*. Translated by Harris Rackham. Cambridge, London: Harvard University Press, W. Heinemann, 1947.

Appadurai, Arjun. "Introduction: Commodities and the Politics of Value." In *The Social Life of Things: Commodities in Cultural Perspective*, edited by Arjun Appadurai, 3–63. Cambridge: Cambridge University Press, 1992.

Barthes, Roland. *Elements of Semiology*. Translated by Annette Lavers and Colin Smith. London: Cape, 1969.

Barthes, Roland. *Mythologies*. Translated by Richard Howard and Annette Lavers. New York: Hill and Wang, 2012.

Barthes, Roland. "The Death of the Author." In *Image—Music—Text*, selected and translated by Stephen Heath, 142–148. London: Fontana Press, 1977.

Barthes, Roland. "The Rhetoric of the Image." In *Image—Music—Text*, selected and translated by Stephen Heath, 32–51. London: Fontana Press, 1977.

Bartky, Sandra Lee. *Femininity and Domination: Studies in the Phenomenology of Oppression*. London, New York: Routledge, 1990.

Bartky, Sandra Lee. "Foucault, Feminity, and the Modernization of Patriarchal Power." In *Feminism and Foucault: Reflections on Resistance*, edited by Irene Diamond, and Lee Quinby, 61–78. Boston: Northeastern University Press, 1988.

Beck, Urlich. *Risk Society: Towards a New Modernity*, Translated by Mark Ritter. London: Sage, 1992.

Bell, David, and Gill Valentine. *Consuming Geographies: We Are Where We Eat*. London, New York: Routledge, 1997.

Bogataj, Janez. "Hitra prehrana—dediščina in sodobnost" [Fast Food—Heritage and Modernity]. In *Hitra hrana* [Fast Food], edited by Dražigost Pokorn, 7–20. Ljubljana: Inštitut za higieno, MF, 1997.

Bourdieu, Pierre. "Language and Symbolic Power", translated by Gino Raymond and Matthew Adamson. In *The Discourse Reader*, edited by Adam Jaworski, and Nikolas Coupland, 502–513. London, New York: Routledge, 1999.

Bourdieu, Pierre. *Practical Reason: On the Theory of Action*. Translated by Randal Johnson. Stanford: Stanford University Press, 1998.

Caglar, Ayse. "McDoner: Doner Kebap and the Social Positioning Struggle of German Turks." In *Marketing in a Multicultural World: Ethnicity, Nationalism, and Cultural Identity*, edited by Janeen Arnold Costa and Gary J. Bamossy, 209–230. Thousand Oaks: Sage, 1995.

Carroll, Lewis. *Alice's Adventures in Wonderland and Through the Looking-Glass*. Twickenham: Tiger, 1993.

Culler, Jonathan. *Saussure*. Hassocks, Sussex: The Harvester Press, 1976.

Derrida, Jacques. *Of Grammatology*. Translated by Gayatri Chakravorty Spivak. Baltimore, London: The Johns Hopkins University Press, 1976.

Dietler, Michael. "Introduction: Embodied Material Culture." *Archaeological Review from Cambridge* 20/2 (2005): 3–5.

Dreyfus, Hubert L., and Paul Rabinow. *Michel Foucault: Beyond Structuralism and Hermeneutics*. Chicago: The University of Chicago Press, 1982.

Dolar, Mladen. "Spremna beseda" [Foreword]. In Michel Foucault, *Vednost—oblast—subject* [Knowledge—Power—Subject], vii–xxxv. Ljubljana: Krt, 1991.

Dolar, Mladen. *Prozopopeja* [Prosopopoeia]. Ljubljana: Analecta, 2006.

Douglas, Mary, and Baron Isherwood. *The World of Goods: Towards an Anthropology of Consumption*. London, New York: Routledge, 1996.

Fairclough, Norman. *Discourse and Social Change*. Cambridge, Oxford: Polity Press, Blackwell, 1992.

Falk, Pasi. *The Consuming Body*. London: Sage, 1994.

Fanon, Frantz. "The Negro and Psychopathology." In *Identity: A Reader*, edited by Paul du Gay, Jessica Evans, and Peter Redman, 202–221. London: Open University, Sage, 2000.

Feyerabend, Paul. *Against Method*. London: Verso, 1975.

Fiske, John. *Introduction to Communication Studies*. London: Routledge, 1990.

Foucault, Michel. *Discipline and Punish: The Birth of the Prison*. Translated by Alan Sheridan. New York: Pantheon Books, 1977.

Foucault, Michel. "Truth and Power," translated by Colin Gordon. In *Power/Knowledge: Selected Interviews and Other Writings, 1972–1977*, edited by Colin Gordon, 109–133. New York: Pantheon Books, 1980.

Foucault, Michel. "The Confession of the Flesh," translated by Colin Gordon. In *Power/Knowledge: Selected Interviews and Other Writings, 1972–1977*, edited by Colin Gordon, 194–228. New York: Pantheon Books, 1980.

Foucault, Michel. "What is an Author?" translated by Donald F. Bouchard and Sherry Simon. In *Language, Counter-memory, Practice: Selected Essays and Interviews by Michel Foucault*, edited by Donald F. Bouchard, 113–138. New York: Cornell University Press, 1980.

Foucault, Michel. "The Order of Discourse," translated by Ian McLeod. In *Untying the Text: A Post-Structuralist Reader*, edited by Robert Young, 51–76. Boston: Routledge, Kegan Paul, 1981.

Foucault, Michel. "The Subject and Power," translated by Leslie Sawyer. In *Michel Foucault: Beyond Structuralism and Hermeneutics*, edited by Hubert L. Dreyfus and Paul Rabinow, 208–226. New York: Harvester Wheatsheaf, 1983.

Foucault, Michel. *The History of Sexuality. Vol. 1. The Will to Knowledge*. Translated by Robert Hurley. New York: Vintage Books, 1990.

Foucault, Michel. *The Archaeology of Knowledge*. Translated by A. M. Sheridan Smith. London, New York: Routledge, 2002.

Giddens, Anthony. *The Consequences of Modernity*. Cambridge: Polity Press, 1990.

Godina Golija, Maja. *Prehrana v Mariboru v dvajsetih in tridesetih letih 20. stoletja* [Eating Habits in Maribor in the Nineteen-Twenties and Thirties]. Maribor: Založba Obzorja, 1996.

Grdina, Igor. *Vladarji, lakaji, bohemi* [Rulers, Footmen, Boheminas]. Ljubljana: Studia Humanitatis, 2001.

Hall, Stuart. "The Work of Representation." In *Representation: Cultural Representations and Signifying Practices*, edited by Stuart Hall, 13–74. Sage: London, 2002.

Hall, Stuart. "The Spectacle of the 'Other.'" In *Representation: Cultural Representations and Signifying Practices*, edited by Stuart Hall, 233–290. Sage: London, 2002.

Hebdige, Dick. *Subculture: The Meaning of Style*. London, New York: Methuen & Co., 1979.

Jaworski, Adam, and Nikolas Coupland. "Introduction: Perspectives on Discourse Analysis." In *The Discourse Reader*, edited by Adam Jaworski and Nikolas Coupland, 1–44. Routledge: London, New York, 1999.

Kamin, Tanja. "Promocija zdravja kot mit opolnomočenega državljana" [The Promotion of Health as the Myth of the Empowered Citizen]. PhD diss., University of Ljubljana, 2004.

Kantorowicz, Ernst H. *The King's Two Bodies: A Study in Mediaeval Political Theology*. Princeton: Princeton University Press, 1970.

Laclau, Ernesto, and Chantal Mouffe. *Hegemony and Socialist Strategy: Towards a Radical Democratic Politics*. London, New York: Verso, 2001.

Laclau, Ernesto, and Chantal Mouffe. "Post-Marxism Without Apologies." In *New Reflections on the Revolution of Our Time*, edited by Ernesto Laclau, 97–130. London, New York: Verso, 1990.

Levi-Strauss, Claude. *The Savage Mind*. Translated by George Weidenfeld. Chicago: The University of Chicago Press, 1966.

Lupton, Deborah. *Food, the Body and the Self*. London: Sage, 1996.

Marx, Karl. *Capital: A Critique of Political Economy.Volume I: The Process of Capitalist Production, by Karl Marx*. Translated from the 3rd German edition, by Samuel Moore and Edward Aveling, edited by Federick Engels. Revised and amplified according to the 4th German edition by Ernest Untermann. Chicago: Charles H. Kerr and Co., 1909.

Marx, Karl. *The Eighteenth Brumaire of Louis Bonaparte*. Moscow: Progress Publishers, 1967.

Mauss, Marcel. *The Gift: The forms and Functions of Exchange in Archaic Societies*. Translated by Ian Cunnison. London: Cohen and West Ltd., 1954.

McGuigan, Jim. *Cultural Populism*. London, New York: Routledge, 1993.

Miller, Daniel. *Material Culture and Mass Consumption*. Oxford, New York: Blackwell, 1987.

Miller, Daniel. "Artefacts and the Meaning of Things." In *Companion Encyclopedia of Anthropology*, edited by Tim Ingold, 396–419. London, New York: Routledge, 1994.

Minnich, Robert G. "The gift of koline and the articulation of identity in Slovene." *Glasnik SED* 27/3–4 (1987): 171–179.

Močnik, Rastko. "Studia humanitatis danes [Studia Humanitatis Today]." In *Retorika Starih / Elementi semiologije* [Ancient Rhetoric / Elements of Semiology] by Roland Barthes, 211–238. Ljubljana: Studia humanitatis, 1990.

Nietzsche, Friedrich. *Beyond Good and Evil: Prelude to the Philosophy of the Future*. Translated by Judith Norman. Cambridge: Cambridge University Press, 2002.

Ohnuki-Tierney, Emiko. *Rice as Self: Japanese Identities through Time*. Princeton: Princeton University Press, 1993.

Said, Edward W. *Orientalism*. London: Penguin, 2003.

Saussure, Ferdinand de. *Course on General Linguistics*. Edited by Charles Bally and Albert Sechehaye with the collaboration of Albert Riedlinger, translated and annotated by Roy Harris. New York: Philosophical Library, 1959.

Scholliers, Peter. "Meals, Food Naratives, and Sentiments of Belonging in Past and Present." In *Food, Drink and Identity in Europe Since the Middle Ages*, edited by Peter Scholliers, 3–23. Berg, Oxford, 2001.

Sobal, Jeffrey. "Sociological Analysis of the Stigmatisation of Obsesity." In *A Sociology of Food and Nutrition: The Social Appetite*, edited by Lauren Williams and John Germov, 187–204. South Melbourne: Oxford University Press, 1999.

Stankovič, Peter. "Rokerji s konca tisočletja" [Rockers at the End of the Millennium]. In *Urbana plemena. Subkulture v Sloveniji v devetdesetih* [Urban Tribes: Subcultures in Slovenia in the Nineties], edited by Peter Stankovič, Gregor Tomc, and Mitja Velikonja, 43–52. Ljubljana: Študentska založba, 1999.

Stankovič, Peter. "Burek? Ja, bitte!" *Dnevnik, Zelena pika*, January 15, 2005, 36–37.

Stariha, Gorazd. "'Dvigam to čašo za bratstvo in enotnost naših narodov'" ['I raise this Cup to the Brotherhood and Unity of our Nations']. *Zgodovina za vse* 13/2 (2006): 83–114.

Šurk, Barbara. "Mahmud Ahmadinežad" [Mahmoud Ahmadinejad]. *Delo, Sobotna priloga*, July 2, 2005, 3.

Tivadar, Blanka. "Hrana kot simbolna potrošnja" [Food as Symbolic Consumption]. PhD diss., University of Ljubljana, 1998.

Todorova, Marija. *Imagining the Balkans.* New York: Oxford University Press, 2009.

Toš, Niko, and Brina Malnar. "Stališča o zdravju in zdravstvu: analiza rezultatov raziskav iz obdobja 1994–2001" [Views of Health and Healthcare: An Analysis of Research Results in the Period 1994–2001]. In *Družbeni vidiki zdravja* [Social Aspects of Health], edited by Niko Toš and Brina Malnar, 87–161. Ljubljana, FDV, IDV, Center za raziskovanje javnega mnenja in množičnih komunikacij, 2002.

Van Leeuwen, Theo. *Discourse and Practice: New Tools for Critical Discourse Analysis.* Oxford, New York: Oxford University, 2008.

Vogrinc, Jože. "Raymond Williams in navadna kultura [Raymond Williams and Ordinary Culture]." In *Navadna kultura: izbrani spisi* [Ordinary Culture: Selected Essays] by Raymond Williams, 289–303. Ljubljana: Studia humanitatis, 1998.

Weedon, Chris. *Feminist Practice and Poststructuralist Theory.* Oxford, New York: Basil Blackwell, 1987.

White, Kevin. *An Introduction to the Sociology of Health and Illness.* London: Sage, 2002.

Williams, Lauren, and John Germov. "The Thin Ideal: Women, Food, and Dieting." In *A Sociology of Food and Nutrition: The Social Appetite,* edited by Lauren Williams and John Germov, 205–227. South Melbourne: Oxford University Press, 1999.

Williams, Raymond. "Base and Superstructure in Marxist Cultural Theory." *Culture and Materialism: Selected Essays,* 31–49.London: Verso, 2005.

Wittgenstein, Ludwig. *Philosophical Investigations.* Translated by Gertrude Elizabeth Margaret Anscombe. Oxford: Basil Blackwell, 1958.

Burekindex

For Product Safety Concerns and Information please contact our EU representative GPSR@taylorandfrancis.com Taylor & Francis Verlag GmbH, Kaufingerstraße 24, 80331 München, Germany

Batch number: 10370533

Printed by Printforce, the Netherlands